MW01126002

Dear Dewey:

A Year in the Life of a High School Teacher

Max Shelnutt

Copyright © 2019 Maxwell O. Shelnutt
All rights reserved
ISBN 9781074037123

Cover picture, "Saum School, County Highway 23, Saum, Beltrami County, MN";
Public Domain. Library of Congress. Retrieved from picryl.com.

Unless otherwise noted, Scripture quotations are taken from *The Holy Bible, New American Standard, Updated Edition*. Copyright 1996; by The Lockman Foundation. Used by permission. All rights reserved

Table of Contents

Dear Dewey

Introduction

For many years, I have thought about keeping a log, a diary of sorts, of my life as a teacher. For some reason, I thought others might like to know what it's like to be an educator in today's world, from the perspective of one who actually lives it. It seems weekly there are headlines indicting teachers who have crossed lines and done horrific things, and articles about the state of education in our society from the data-driven talking heads. It has always been my hope that if I got around to writing down my tale, it would be informative, thought-provoking, sobering, humorous, and most of all, genuine.

It should be known that while this volume is set up as a diary, and is organized as a year in my life, it is actually culled from many years of teaching. While all the parts of the stories are true, they are often compilations of various experiences, not from the same year, and certainly not from the same school site. It should also be noted that it is not my intention to demean anyone, and as such, the identities of individuals are protected as best as I could provide. With the exception of those from whom I've received permission, all names are fictitious.

3

Some of my readers might wonder about the title, *Dear Dewey*. As I've already stated, I wanted to format this book as a diary. I address my entries to Dewey instead of the classic, "Dear Diary" as a nod to John Dewey. Dewey was an education reformer in the latter part of the 19th century, into the 20th century. While his theories have both supporters and detractors, his fingerprints are still evident on today's educational system. The good news is that one does not need to plumb the depths of Dewey's thoughts to enjoy and appreciate this book.

Although these anecdotes are inspired by my life and will be informative for some, at the heart of every entry is a story; some longer than others. If there is any value and enjoyment in these stories, some credit should be given to three men in my life. My introduction to storytelling came from my father, James "Jim" Shelnutt. He was one of the most intelligent men I've ever known, relatively quiet, and not one who wished to draw attention to himself or be the life of the party. But when he was called upon to speak in front of a crowd, or he was telling a story, he commanded attention and held the room spellbound. Years later, the good Lord brought into my life a spiritual father of sorts. Fr. Thom Smith showed me the importance of story. That is, through his example, I saw the power and value of story. He also shed light on the need to never lose the humanity of the tale. Folks, plain and simple, are amusing, and will likely reflect some nuance of each of our beings. Thom and my father had much in common, even beyond storytelling. I wish they had met at some point. Lastly, I cannot overstate the contribution my buddy John Alberti has made in my yarn spinning. We met when I was in high school, maybe early college, and have been writing together, formally and informally, ever since. It's been John's turn of phrase, vocabulary, timing, and rhythm of speech that still amuses me to this day. He has helped me more than he knows.

Finally, I feel the need to acknowledge a few individuals who have made this journey possible. First, my wife Chau (rhymes with "Joe"). She has been my biggest supporter from our first date so many years ago. Second, I thank Lou Booth and Tony Gavia for listening to me gripe over the years. They provided redirection when I needed it and words of empathy when needed. I also want to thank Monica Gavia for her encouragement in writing. She has been a great cheerleader and resource before, during, and after the composition of these pages.

As you might have noticed, this book has been self-published. While it has been combed through several times, it might be imperfect—just like me. If you find typos, or a verb tense agreement issues, it's likely not because I am ignorant, but rather that I am lazy and impatient.

And to all my friends on social media who have told me relentlessly, "You should write a book," well, here it is. You'd better buy it and read it. And pick up a few more copies—they make great last minute gifts.

August

Education is not preparation for life; education is life itself.

– John Dewey

Dear Dewey,

As I begin this journey, and the reader with me, I feel compelled to ask, "Did you read the Introduction? Really?" I used to skip over that part, too, until I was assigned to read a book entitled, *How to Read a Book*. A book on how to read a book? Sounds circular and self-serving. It was here that I was convinced that all that front-end stuff was important. If you have not read it, go back and do so right now. I truly believe it will give you a better experience with the remainder of this book, and will provide you with some insights that you would not glean otherwise. Besides, I took the time to write it, so …

Skipping over introductory material must be in the human genome. At the very least, most folks are not convinced of its value from the earliest points of our education. For example, I reuse most of my tests. That is, I do not make fresh copies every year, but rather try to save the district some money by reusing the same exams. Since many of my tests include matching and multiple choice questions, the first words in the directions are, "Do not write on this test." After giving a few of these tests, the first few words now look like, "***DO NOT WRITE ON THIS TEST!***" I even draw this to my students' attention before passing the tests out. Still, I get students who will circle their answer on the exam, despite the fact that I've also given them an answer document where they are to "bubble in" their answers.

So, don't be THAT student. Go back and read the Introduction. We'll still be here when you get back.

Dear Dewey,

Last week was Freshmen Orientation Day. This is a day when the incoming class plays some games with current student leaders and is shown the ins and outs of the campus. A former student (now a senior) was escorting two freshmen girls around the school grounds and decided to drop into my classroom. He introduced the girls to me while they were looking wide-eyed at all the things I have on my walls (they're virtually covered floor to ceiling). One of the girls asked, "What do you teach?" I encouraged her to study the material hanging about and tell me what she thought I taught. She looked for moment and said with all seriousness, "Comedy?"

Folks who see my room either love it or feel like it is just too much. I have only heard positive things, but I assume that those who do not like it just remain silent. The first time I walked into my classroom so many years ago, I was struck by one feature: no windows. The gentleman who had the classroom before me was a long term substitute who had conducted class for most of the first semester. Under the circumstances, he did a stellar job. When I took over the room, I saw bland walls that were badly in need of a fresh coat of paint. I also noticed about four or five pieces of copier paper taped to the walls. Upon closer examination I realized they were colored drawings of windows done by the students. The long term sub figured if they could not have actual windows they could at least have imaginary ones.

I think I started with a half dozen or so posters of varying sizes, with some of those recovered from a pile of discarded posters in the faculty workroom. The collection has grown over the years, and with every changing year I try to add something fresh, replacing some older posters, to give the students varied visuals to see and look forward to. It amuses me how there will always be a few students who in the spring will see something new to them, convinced that it has not been there since August.

Dear Dewey,

Today was the first day of the new school year. As I stood at the door to welcome my Advanced Placement (A.P.) World History class, the first student walked through the doorway. I could not help but notice the textbook he was carrying.

Me: "Hey! Are you in the right class? That's an A.P. US History text."
Student: "It's an A.P. US History text?"

Me: "Yep. This here is an A.P. World textbook." [I show him the correct book]

Student: "Huh. That would explain why I had such a hard time answering the questions on the summer assignment."

Only 179 more teaching days until the end of the school year.

Dear Dewey,

Having gotten through the official duties of the first day such as seating charts and going over the syllabi, I wanted to start Day 2 on a bit less formal footing with the students. I just never know how it is going to go when I give the proverbial mic to the audience.

Me: "Hey, welcome back everybody. Did anyone do anything exciting over the summer?"

Student: "Well, my turtle had his leg amputated."

What could I say? His summer topped mine by a mile.

Dear Dewey,

Today concluded the first complete week with my student teacher, Joan. She is in the first phase of her program. It was also the first unit test for my students. Some classes did well, others did not.

I'm guessing Joan took the poor showing personally. Having written the grade data for each class on the board (how many A's, B's, etc.), she circled the number of failures with great emphasis, damaging beyond repair one of my white board markers. A few of the under-performing students chuckled. I have seen this numerous times in the past. It is a kind of deflective response; not wanting to own their laziness in preparing for the test. Joan pounded on the board with the marker, firmly saying, "You think this is funny? You think THIS is funny?!?" In my mind I urged Joan to dial it down, but did not say a word so as not to embarrass her. I'm guessing a couple of students made a comment because she continued her tirade with, "I don't want any excuses. Excuses are bullshit!" That was soon followed-up with, "And opinions are like assholes–everyone has one." I waited until class was over to let Joan know that it's just not acceptable to yell "bullshit" at a bunch of fifteen year olds; maybe when they are seniors, but not sophomores. I saw it as a teachable moment.

Dear Dewey,

Today's interchange with some students:

Student A: "Wow! It's freezing in here (i.e. classroom)."

Me: "Yep."

Student B: "Is it always this cold in here?"

Me: "Yep. I was raised in a mortuary, so I like it this cold."

Look of uncertainty from the students.

Truth be told, I prefer the room cooler than warmer for a couple reasons. First, I drink coffee throughout the day. As such, my inner body temperature seems to run on the warmer side. It is like I have my own little furnace burning inside me. Students will show up to my classroom with a throw blanket, and I am standing there with sweat stains under my arms as if I had just gone 15 rounds with Ali. The students can always put on another layer; I can only take off so many layers, legally.

The other reason is actually for the students' well-being. A cooler room seems to help their alertness. If the room leans more on the warmer side, they get lulled to drowsiness. I would prefer to find a happy medium, but our HVAC system is not that dialed in. Throw in thirty-five bodies and it's nearly impossible to regulate.

Dear Dewey,

Got home from a full week and started to prepare dinner. As I was shucking the sweet corn (yes, we hand-shuck our corn here in the Shelnutt household; we come from a long line of hand-shuckers), one of the ears of corn had a little baby corn inside it. I was quite surprised. I thought the only pregnant thing in this house was … … … the long pauses in my conversation.

Dear Dewey,

Early on in my professional career, I realized that the dark side of human nature reigns in many of my students. Yes, given the opportunity, some students will choose to cheat instead of accepting the consequences of their failure to study. This practice is as old as time. I'm pretty sure Cain copied off Abel when Eve homeschooled them. Cain then killed Abel after Abel tried to cover up his answers. (Okay, so maybe I wasn't paying attention the day that story was taught in Sunday school).

Many of my tests are embarrassingly easy. I often base them off the worksheets the students have done, and I tell them so. In essence, they have the test and answers in advance. Multiple choice and matching, most typically. Students will try so many ways to cheat, but usually it involves writing on the hand, scribbles on the desk, or in this modern age, photos of the worksheets on their phones. But more times than not, a student who hasn't really embraced the whole school thing just shows up to class and proclaims to the class, "Oh shit, is there a test today?" I will then point to the words on the board that has informed them of this for the past ten days, and remind the student that I have mentioned it every day for the last week. The student panics because he or she had not taken the time to write anything on his/her hand.

It is because of the latter type of cheating student that I use different versions of the test. The questions will be the same, but the order will be changed. I'm not trying to get a "gotcha" moment with my students. I tell them in advance that there are different versions. My desire is that this will discourage them from cheating by looking on someone else's answer sheet.

Today my seniors had their first test of the semester with me. Since I also teach sophomores and juniors in other courses, about half my class has had me before and knows the drill. Unfortunately for Mike, he was new to my approach and had all but checked-out as a student some time in his junior year. After taking attendance I got the students to clear off their desks and laps (where they keep their backpacks), and handed out the tests. I presort the tests to make sure that for any given student, the tests to their left/right and front/back are different. Students do not realize it, but their body language is what almost always gives them away when they are cheating. Such was the case with Mike. I can only guess that this was not his first time at taking the short cut to a passing grade, but for a seasoned pro, his skills were left wanting.

After everyone had turned in their tests, there was enough time for me to quickly correct them in class. Having done so, I decided to let each student know how they had done. I give the students three choices when I call out their names: say, "yes" to have me read their test result out for all to hear: say, "no" and wait to see it on the online grade book: or come up and have me show it to them privately. I was going through the list when it came to Mike's name. I called out his name. Knowing the girl he copied from got a 90%, he replied with a confident, "Yes!" I said, "Yes?" to make sure I had heard him correctly. He confirmed with a heartier, "Yes!" I stated a somewhat digging, "5%." His buddies busted out with a spontaneous taunting laugh. He asked me if he had heard correctly. "5?" "Yes," I assured, "a

5." I continued with the rest of the students, noticing all the while the look of confusion on Mike's face.

After I finished giving all the students their test results, Mike came up telling me for all to hear that I must have graded it incorrectly. I showed him the test, and invited him to show me which ones I had mistakenly marked wrong. He looked at the test with the same blank stare as when I first gave it to him at the beginning of class. He couldn't tell me where I was in error since he didn't know the material. "Well, let me see someone else's test. Let me compare it to theirs." As the rest of the students watched and listened as this drama unfolded, I told Mike I could not do that due to privacy issues. As he walked back to his seat I mentioned, "Besides, it wouldn't matter. There are different tests, so the answers would be different." As he sat down he said, "There are different tests?" I said that there were, and that I had told the class that well in advance. "Mike, you had the right answers, just the wrong test."

In my own expression of the dark side of human nature, I wanted to take a dig at Mike's obvious stumble, but his buddies gave him a verbal lashing laced with sardonic mockeries far beyond anything I could have composed. I trust Mike won't be cheating on the next test. I also hope he understands that I have a greater respect for someone who tries on their own merit and gets only 45%, than one who cheats in some fashion, and gets 90%.

Dear Dewey,

"I want to live until I die. I want to be advanced at love and I really want to bring joy and laughter into the world, even if it's after I'm gone." (Michael Cheshire: author, spiritual leader, humorist, and serial entrepreneur—per his website.) I think this is one of the things that keeps me getting up every morning at 5:15 and driving forty-five miles each way to teach ... the laughter.

Dear Dewey,

Last night was Back-to-School Night. It is one of two required evening events for teachers, the other being Open House. Depending on what I happen to be teaching that year, I may get a room full of parents, or just one. Generally speaking, my sophomore A.P. World classes get quite a few parents attending. This is their child's first go at an A.P. class, so they have a lot of questions and anxieties. On the other end of the spectrum are the parents of my senior class, Government/Economics. I might get one or two, and they might just pop in for a minute. By the time parents have a child who is a senior, they pretty much know the score and do not see the need to sit through another evening of classroom policies, which are usually spelled out in the course syllabus that is sent home at the beginning of the semester.

I have a lot of posters on my walls, and a few items placed here and there. My collection has grown over the years, and I hope I keep it somewhat interesting for the students. One set of items that I have had for some time are five cereal boxes affixed to my wall. These are from the "monster cereals" put out by General Mills (think "Count Chocula" and the like). Parents and students always ask why I have them. It provides me the opportunity to explain how they are there to illustrate a marketing strategy (since they only come out a couple months during the year). Most parents grant me an affirming nod once they hear the explanation.

One of my other items is a black crow that I picked up around Halloween time at one of those "only a dollar" stores. I found a great place to "perch" him on the top of the television hanging in one corner of my room. I find it funny when at the end of the year I will have a student suddenly notice the bird and ask how long it has been there. They cannot believe it was there all year long. Well, during Back-to-School Night one of the mothers noticed it. During the last few minutes when I open it up for questions she asked with a hint of disdain in her voice, "What is that bird doing up there?" I smiled and said it really did not serve a purpose; it was random. With all the bitterness she could muster, the mother said under her breath for us all to hear, "It sure is." As the time expired and the parents were moving on to the next class, one of the other mothers smiled and let me know she liked the bird. At least we ended on a high note.

Most people don't realize what it takes to put on a Back-to-School Night. The teachers have their various responsibilities as it relates to their room and classes, but there are many other behind-the-scene details that must be addressed. This is usually relegated to one of the VPs. As I saw the administrator who was in charge of this year's evening, I asked how it went. He felt it went well, and indicated that he had made some notes as to how to improve it next year. A broad smile came on his face as he told me that he had just received an email from a parent who was unable to make it the previous night. This parent asked if the school could put on another Back-to-School Night this year so she could attend. Don't worry, there will be another one coming around in about 364 days.

Dear Dewey,

Today was Picture Day. Not only do the students get their portraits taken, but so do the teachers. These photos will be ones that can be ordered in special "packets," and will also be included in the yearbook. Some teachers just show up with whatever they happen to be wearing that day. Others will give some concerted thought, especially if they are looking to don a silly outfit. I usually wear a shirt and tie, though I have gone less formal a couple of times. This year I decided to go a bit "old school" and wear a blazer with my shirt and tie.

I went to get my portrait done a few minutes before the start of the school day to get ahead of the first group of students that would be getting their snapshots taken. As I walked up to the photographer, he looked me over once and stated, "You must be the principal." I assured him I was not. He glared over the top of his glasses, scanning my expression for signs of jesting.

He led me to "the spot" where I was to stand. It was fairly obvious, as there were footprints on the ground letting you know exactly where you were to be. To make it a bit less clear, there were two sets of prints; one orange, and the other blue. Since the photographer didn't say which to go with, I decided to split it down the middle and picked one of each. I am assuming this choice accounts for the awkward look that I have in my finished photo.

The photographer proceeded with the customary directions of how I was to be positioned. I am convinced they do this solely to justify their jobs and title as a "professional photographer." After much turning slightly this way and that, tilting here and there, and holding a smile for what seemed like the entirety of a Martin Scorsese film, the picture was taken. Glad that's over. Wait! Apparently there is a slight glare coming from my glasses. Repeat all of the above. Let's try that again. After four attempts, we were both done. We went with the first picture. I highly doubt a single student, when looking over her yearbook twenty years from now in a moment of reminiscing, will stop and comment, "Dr. Shelnutt was a fun teacher, but look at that glare coming off his left lens. What was he thinking?"

Dear Dewey,

When I was a kid, my buddies and I played with baseball cards. No, we weren't hardcore collectors or anything (some even ended up flicking in the spokes of our bike tire spokes). We had our stack that we would take to school with us, and we "flipped" them. That is, we had a game we would play against one another. The winner got to keep the cards. I suppose this was our generation's version of marbles.

During the same time, my sister had what I believe were called "Clackers." Basically, two acrylic balls on the end of a string which, when used properly, allowed the two spheres to clack together. Sure, a few of them unexpectedly shattered, but they were fun.

I started thinking about those old fads when I saw my students in a "competition" during lunch today. The students take a common plastic water bottle, which still has water in it, and flip it, seeing who can make it land upright on the desk without it falling over. Simple and addictive, but irritating in the middle of class. I have observed many fads over the years since I have been teaching: Slap bracelets, Garbage Pail Kids cards, Tamagotchis, and Silly Bands to mention a few. By definition, fads come and go like the wind. That said, there are three that I recall from over the decades of my teaching career that stand out to me.

The first fad I recall as a teacher consisted of round, flat pieces of cardboard called "Pogs." I first saw Pogs, or the more generic name "milk caps," when I was vacationing in Hawaii. My nephew was playing with them and I thought, "This would be a huge hit in California." I should have jumped on that thought because within six months of returning to the state, milk caps were all the rage. I had brought a few back with me to show my students, and there was a little interest, especially from the boys. Within a year or two, these same boys couldn't give them away. Large boxes of milk caps and the required accessories could be seen at garage sales everywhere.

The next fad, and the one that had me scratching my head the most, was the pacifier phase. Yep, pacifiers. My female students (I never saw a male student with one) began to wear pacifiers at the end of cords around their necks. I recently saw a video of Joan Jett performing her hit, "I Love Rock n Roll," wearing a silver pacifier around her neck, but that was the early 80's. This fad hit sometime in the 90's. It wasn't just ornamental, either. Some of these girls would start sucking on their pacifiers in the middle of a lesson. Not terribly disruptive, but a bit disturbing.

Just before the current water bottle frenzy was the fidget spinner period. These things seemed to appear overnight. They do make a bit of sound, but not so much so as to take away from the learning environment. They were mostly a problem before class began as a student was showing off his latest acquisition. It caught the imagination of our students so much that they began making them in one of the classes at school. One design was patterned after the Batman insignia. Knowing how much I like the Dark Knight, one of the students, showing me the new gadget, asked if I wanted him to make me one. I thought that would be very cool, even if I never used the thing. Then he told me the price; I thought he was going to make it for me pro bono. I told him I would think about it.

Sometimes I tell my students about the "Pet Rock" fad. I never had one, but I recall it vividly. The students get a kick out of it and without fail ask, "How could people be so stupid?" Oh, you just wait

and see what YOUR kids bring home.

September

An investment in knowledge pays the best interest.

– Benjamin Franklin

Dear Dewey,

Got home from the first day of the new month. I arrived exhausted, my feet aching, and my voice raw, but I had to cook dinner. It felt a bit warm in the kitchen, but I assumed it was due to preparing the meal. After dinner I decided to clean up for the night and then rest a bit. As I stood at my mirror, I could feel and see just how much I was sweating. Have I contracted malaria? Do I have the plague? I went and checked the thermostat. It was there that I discovered that my wife, who thought she had turned on the AC earlier in the day, had in reality turned on the heater. On the plus side, I dropped two pounds and will have a lower energy bill than expected

Dear Dewey,

In trying to reassure one student who is on the shorter side, another student chimes in:

Me: "My wife is only 4'10"."

Student: "Your wife is only 4'10"?"

Me: "Yep, 4'10"."

Student: "Wow! 4'10". Really? How tall is that?"

Me: "I'm pretty sure it's right around 4'10"."

Dear Dewey,

As I was reading a weekly magazine that features a section on the etymology of words, I found out the scientific name for French kissing is "cataglottism." Seems like a foolproof way of making sure you go home alone. "Hey baby, what say you and me go back to my place for a little cataglottism." Doesn't quite have the same appeal. This is one reason I discourage my students from going on to major in Science.

Dear Dewey,

While I was winding down one of my classes today, it occurred to me, "This IS my circus, and these ARE my monkeys!"

It is something to see the degree to which teachers take students under their wings (sorry for the mixed metaphors). I think society pretty much expects that with elementary school teachers, especially in the early grades. Most early educators are female, and these teachers tend to be very nurturing. But listen to some middle school and high school teachers talk. Rarely do you hear them refer to their students as "those students" or the very generic, "the students." It is almost always "my students" or "my kids." This is why it hurts so deeply when those of us in the profession are accused of anything less than wanting the best for the students placed in our charge. In many cases, sadly, we spend more time on a daily basis with Johnny and Jane than do their parents. This is not always the fault of the parents, as some have to work evening shifts, or in some cases, two jobs just to pay the bills.

These are not always the best circumstances, but they are our reality, and we will work alongside parents to nurture their children— our kids. We hope to send them home each day a bit further along on their journey as better people. Sending them back from our loving circus.

Dear Dewey,

Worked with my World History students (sophomores) on their first mapping exercise. I have found that most of my students don't get the concept of a map "key," so I demonstrated on the board what theirs might look like for this map. The symbols had to represent a water battle and land battle. For the water battle I drew a simple boat with a sail. For the land battle I drew a cannon. As soon as I finished my simple cannon, I realized it resembled the male reproductive organ (and no, I'm not talking about a glass of wine). The more I tried to add to it so that it looked more like a cannon, the worse it got. I thought it best not to draw attention to it by erasing it, but realized students were beginning to grin and whisper. Acting quickly I said, "Or you could just use a simpler symbol like a star, to show an explosion from a battle." There was an immediate outcry, "Why did you erase the cannon thing, Dr. Shelnutt?" Ah, so glad I get to work with and shape tomorrow's leaders.

Dear Dewey,

In my senior classes (Government and Economics) I often allow time to discuss significant current events. Since today is September 11, I decided to take some time to talk about that day. None of my students were born when the events occurred back in 2001. I started by telling them how there will be significant incidents in their lives, maybe only one or two, which they will always remember where there were when they heard about it. For some older adults, it was when JFK was assassinated. For others, it might have been a positive event, like the first lunar landing in 1969. For me, it was 9/11.

I explained how and when I initially heard of the first plane, and then the second. I had just begun my studies at seminary, and was sitting in Beginning Greek class. How I sat in dismay when later that day I saw the images on the evening news; it was surreal. I further shared how, as one who grew up in New York, everyone I knew from there was touched/connected by the events personally in some manner. I even briefly mentioned how my sister-in-law lost a brother and a cousin. They were both firemen from the same firehouse trying to get people out when the buildings collapsed. Fighting back tears (I try not to "lose it" in front of my students), it was one of those moments when we, my students and I, all felt a little closer to our humanity than our regular class routines affords us.

As a somber air of solemnity hung over the class, out of the still silence came the words, "3,000 people isn't that much." Though I was not shocked when I saw who the student was who made this proclamation, I was still disappointed that anyone, especially someone so young, could be so jaundiced and unfeeling. On the bright side, the remainder of the class was all over her like white on rice. While I don't like to see any student "ganged up on," it was encouraging that so many saw her comment for what it was. She tried to defend it by asking if we all knew how many people there were in the world. I explained how I understood the basic statistical mathematics behind her proposition, but I sought to paint it in more human terms for her. How these people got up that morning with no more desire than to go to work, provide for their families, and return home later that evening, only to have their lives cut short by a faceless enemy. The student stood her ground saying they were stupid for working in the buildings. Somehow, throughout the whole conversation, I never lost my cool. I calmly said that if this were a battle, say in the Civil War where thousands lost their lives, we might think 3,000 is a low number. After all, while we do not like that anyone is killed in war, we understand that a soldier has been placed in harm's way, and dying is a possibility. However, having one's life violently taken while at work in a high-rise building in a large metropolitan city is not what one anticipates. I conveyed that she had her opinion, and that I had mine. Trying to transition smoothly from that to the fundamentals of economic theory was difficult, at least on an emotional level.

It is days like this that make me wonder, even worry, about what tomorrow holds for our society. But then I stop and remind myself that she was only one student out of 35; there were 34 who were appalled by her words. My hope is revived, if only for a moment.

Dear Dewey,

Seeing the blossoming of young love on campus, I was reminded of one of my fondest memories growing up in New York—skate nights with our church youth group. The music, speeding around the rink, hanging out at the snack bar, and the hope of finding that special someone for the "Couple's Skate," all contributed to a night to remember. Recently I came across a short video of that old rink, prior to its final destruction. It was a bittersweet walk down Memory Lane. This precious walk goes out to all those "Couple's Skate" partners I had over the years … both of them.

Dear Dewey,

When I was a student making my way through twelve years of public education, there were certain expectations, including what basic supplies that each student was required to bring to class. At the beginning of the year the teacher would make that list of materials known to the new crop of students, and that list was brought home for the parents to fulfill. The items for elementary school were drastically different from those in the high school, but everyone had a list. In high school, you might end up with five or six lists, one for each subject, but they were pretty much the same: pen, pencil, notebook/binder/folder, perhaps a calculator, notebook paper, and maybe a small planner to write down homework and upcoming tests. We also had until the end of the first week to get our text books covered (which usually consisted of custom fitting them with a brown paper grocery bag).

When I began my teaching career, I had a reasonable list, not unlike the ones from my days as a student. I did find, however, that I "required" certain items that I simply would never hold my students to have. Over time, my "required" items have become "recommended" items. If students want to have just the bare minimum, I suggest they have something with which to write, such as a pen or pencil, and some paper for assignments and note taking. I believe this is not asking too much. It is also my belief that in having the students come to class with these basic items, it serves as a base indicator that they are coming prepared for the day's lesson and work.

When I hand out my syllabus on the first day of class, it includes the recommended supply list. We talk about why each item would be useful in the weeks and months to come. I also include the words, "Note: The classroom teacher does not supply you with these items." Looking back to when I was in school, I don't think I ever considered asking one of my teachers for a pencil or paper, though I might ask another student if, for instance, I just used my last piece of paper or my pen ran out of ink. Now, I have caught some backlash for my policy of not supplying my students with these things, not from the students or parents, but from other educators. Public education, I am reminded, is supposed to be free. This is true, but it is also true that anything the students keep and can take home can have a charge (think supplies in an art or culinary class). I have said to my fellow teachers that by making the students responsible for their own supplies, I am trying to help them, in little ways, to know what it is like to come prepared for whatever job they might have. Their retort was that they, as educators, have never had to pay for their own pen and paper at work. I have actually always had to supply my own, but who wants to quibble over that. My point is that there is so very little that we hold the students responsible for, having something to write with and a piece of paper is fairly entry level accountability. I was even offered some pencils and paper by a retired educator so I could have them available for my students, as if the issue was spending the money out of my own pocket. We clearly are not on the same page on the issue.

The trump card that is usually played in this discussion is that many of the students' parents simply do not take them to get the supplies, or are at the poverty level and cannot afford it. It is true that the demographics of my current district is less than affluent, with a majority of students receiving free or reduced cost lunches. However, when I see a student coming in with nothing to write with, or any paper, on a daily basis, but meanwhile never forgetting to have his $6 mocha and $500 smart phone with him, I have a hard time accepting the "can't afford it" argument.

Having said all that, I do know that there are a few students who probably do struggle to afford the basic supplies of pen and paper. My answer to this situation is not to have those things at the ready in the classroom, but rather to have these supplies at some centrally located place on campus, such as the main office, library, or student store, where students could go before and after school, or at lunch, and get what they needed for class. This would show some initiative on the student's part and enable them to demonstrate responsibility for their own learning, which has been my point all along.

Dear Dewey,

This week is Spirit Week. During Spirit Week, which leads up to "the Big Game," we have different themes for each day. Today was

"Pajama Day." I think we have a pajama day most years; at least every other year. The students, mostly the girls, love this day. I've never seen anything inappropriate ; mostly comfortable leisure wear.

I have a few sets of pajamas I could wear, including a couple of silky ones. Usually I just wear my superhero lounging pants and a Batman shirt (from the classic 60's TV show). If the weather's cool enough, like it was today, I'll wear my robe, too. I get a lot of comments affirming my choice. Today was no different.

As I was handing back graded assignments to my final class of the day, and the robe had been discarded due to the warmth of the afternoon, one student said with approval for all to hear, "I can see you wearing that to bed." Without pausing I replied, "I'm not sure I like the idea of you imagining me in bed." After an initial taunt from his friends, the student smiled through a blushing face and retorted, "That's not what I meant." We all enjoyed the brief moment to be playful with each other. It's moments like this that make the work of learning more of a partnership and a community

Dear Dewey,

Chau (wife): "Your students like you because of your sense of humor, huh?"

Me: "Well, it ain't for my good looks."

Dear Dewey,

Female student blurts out a comment laced with profanity.

Male student immediately follows up with, "Do you kiss your mother with that mouth?"

Female student pounces back with, "Yes I do."

Male student wryly says, "I bet you do."

Dear Dewey,

I was working with my AP US History students asking questions that, based on their assigned reading, they should have known. It wasn't going well. At one point I asked, "Who was opposed to the ratification of the U.S. Constitution?" Silence. Finally one student raised his hand

42

and said, "Jesus?" I laughed at the absurdity of the answer. He immediately followed up his answer with, "Are you going to tell me that Jesus isn't the answer?" Well, he's got me there.

Dear Dewey,

Over the years I have observed that many, though not all, of my "vertically challenged" male students can have quite the attitude problem. In today's society, this is called the "Napoleon Complex" (you know, because he was short and tried to make up for his sense of inadequacies by conquering most of Europe—even though he was not really short, that is just an historical urban legend … but that's a subject for another day).

Tommy was just such a student. His approach to compensating for his perceived shortcomings was to be the class clown and take verbal shots at the teacher. Today Tommy came up behind me while I was at my desk and said, "I can see my future through your glasses." I get it—my glasses are thick, like a crystal ball. Without missing a beat

I said, "I can see your future, too. 'Attention K-Mart shoppers. There is a Blue-Light Special in the jewelry department'." His buddy fell out of his seat laughing. Tommy was less amused.

Dear Dewey,

Today I had one of my "frequent flyers," a student who habitually acts out in a particular manner, take to the skies, so to speak. After several verbal reminders for her to "land" and join the rest of us, I finally asked her to step outside the classroom for a moment. I continued on with the lesson for a few minutes until I got to a point where the students were working on their own. This brief time also gives my flyer a chance to cool down.

I stepped outside in the hall, and thankfully Brenda was still there; otherwise, I would have had to write her up as truant. Calmly, I asked her if she understood how her behavior was disruptive to the general learning environment. Surprisingly, she said she did. If she said she did not, then we'd have had a different issue to address. Since she did know, then the problem was that of intentionally ignoring, or at least indifferent to, her disruptive behavior. She came in and rejoined her class.

For those who, like me for some time, wonder if these students will ever look back on life and have any remorse for how they acted in high school, I believe that at least some will. Just last week I had a former student visit me who happened to be on campus. It has only been a few years, so I still recognized him. As he looked down at his feet, Freddy embarrassingly apologized for how he and other students had acted in my class. He had been a senior at the time. My mind raced back to that class, and in all honesty, his face did not come to mind as being among the real obnoxious types. Sure, he had his fun, but it was within the boundaries I was willing to accept. I tried to assure him that he was not one of my highest flyers, but I did thank him for his kind apology.

Many days this year have been hard, largely due to the crop of students I have. That said, it is at times such as this, when students like

Freddy come back and own their mistakes, that I have hope for people like Brenda, even if they never come back and say a word.

Dear Dewey,

As I was correcting some papers at home, I saw on the news that a couple of people contracted H1N2v after handling a pig. The newscaster reminded viewers to wash their hands after petting animals at the zoo or fair. Isn't that just common sense? I mean, I wash my hands after greeting people at church.

Dear Dewey,

We live in what some would consider a small town (pop. 3,456). I was at our local market, Big Al's, to pick up a few items to complete tonight's dinner. There were two registers open; one with four people, the other with one. Clearly, I took the line with one (momma didn't raise no fool). The older, bearded gentleman in front of me was paying for his purchase which, from what I could surmise, was made up of equal parts bottled water and "adult beverages." Looking at the screen, I saw his total came to $44.04. That must be some special water. The folks in the other line kept looking over. Had I made some kind of breach in the local protocol? As the older customer in front of me was in the midst of paying, I strained to see what all the commotion was about. He had placed a plastic bag on the counter—the type you now get in CA when you pay ten cents per bag. He was paying all right … with pennies; old, oxidized pennies. The reusable bag was full of them. He was counting them out on the conveyor belt, one handful at a time. He must have lost his train of thought because he decided he needed to start all over. To her credit, the young lady at the register, fighting back a bit of laughter over the whole situation, stood there and helped him count. I moved to the other line. I'm pretty sure if I went back right now for an after dinner ice cream run, they'd still be counting out the change.

Dear Dewey,

I was driving on one of the back-roads around here through the orchards to work. Now, in my 38+ years of driving, I've hit many of God's little creatures (unintentional or not is irrelevant to this story). Among the less-than-fortunate have been a variety of birds—mostly pigeons and sparrows. I've had more near-misses than I can recall mostly due to the birds' ability to get out of the way in time. On this particular day I was driving as I normally would when out of the tree tops to my left swooped down a large buzzard. Not only was he big, but he was slow—slower than a sparrow, I assure you. I was genuinely concerned for my windshield. Something is wrong when I have to apply my brakes for a bird. For school children, maybe, but for a dirty ol' bird? (And for those who are wondering, buzzard tastes a lot like peacock.)

Dear Dewey,

I just finished watching a documentary about the life and music of Jaco Pastorius. He was an incredible jazz bassist. That said, I've come to the conclusion that if a movie producer is making a documentary of someone's life, nine times out of ten that individual died a sad, tragic death at a young age. In life, strive to be in the ten percent.

Dear Dewey,

Not a class period goes by that someone doesn't come in and interrupt the class. Now, these are usually legitimate reasons—call slips and passes for students, paperwork from the front office, etc. These are usually delivered by office T.A.'s (Teacher Assistants). For many years now I have kept a bucket of candy in which I keep an assortment of sugary delights. After handing over said call slips, I will usually ask the exiting student, "Do you want some candy?" I've yet to figure out how to make that sound less creepy. I'm still working on it.

Today one of the vice principals was dropping off some information for a number of my students. I must note that the standard protocol for vice principals interrupting a class is as follows: they must always open the door very sheepishly; be somewhat embarrassed that they are breaking in on a secret society; and, lastly, leave just as quickly as they entered. As the VP was leaving, I proclaimed in my best "teacher voice" as if continuing my lecture, "And that, boys and girls, is where babies come from." The humor was not lost on my students who busted out in pure laughter. I'm still waiting for that email letting me know an administrator needs to talk with me in the Administration Office tomorrow.

Dear Dewey,

Today I swung by the office to turn in some paperwork before I left for the day. The end of the day in the office is typically quiet. The phones aren't ringing off the hook, most of the students are gone, and everyone is tired and looking forward to heading home. Just as I walked up to the counter, there was a message coming across the walkie-talkie. I'm not sure who was making the broadcast, but the person was sending out a message to the custodial staff who have the thankless task of getting our entire campus cleaned up and ready for service the next day. "I need someone from custodial services to go to the boy's bathroom over by the 1000 wing. There are two used condoms on the floor. It needs to be cleaned up and the door locked." All of us in the office just looked at each other and broke out with gut-wrenching laughter.

So many things crossed my mind at that moment. First, why were there two? The possible answers to that question were more than I cared to ponder at that time. Somewhere in my head I heard a voice coming over a loud speaker, "Wanda, we need a clean-up in stall three." All things considered, it could have been worse; it could have been the cafeteria. I'm tired. I'm going home.

Dear Dewey

October

I have no special talent. I am only passionately curious.

– Albert Einstein

Dear Dewey,

I don't usually have my students work straight out of the text book, but I did today. I had planned on the class doing a fun activity, a round of "Password", based on vocabulary from the last assigned chapter. However, they did so horrifically poorly on the previous vocabulary exam that I didn't see the point. The students can't give clues about a term when they have no idea what it means.

In lieu of the game, students were to answer summative questions related to our unit on the Early Industrial Revolution. They were to answer thirteen questions, with the first six being "fill-in the blank" and the balance needing to be answered using complete sentences. They found the questions in the text book and were encouraged to use it to answer the questions. One of the questions that required a complete answer was, "Identify three causes of the population explosion that occurred in the 1700s." Most students were able to find the appropriate material in the chapter, but one student simply wrote, "Negatively reduced death." That was it. First, the response is not what I would consider a complete sentence. Second, while it contains three words, it doesn't offer three distinct causes required by the question. Finally, and most baffling, what in the world does his answer mean? How can anything negatively reduce death? What does that look like? Why would reducing death ever be considered a negative thing? And this after nine years of education.

Dear Dewey,

On the way home from work, I went to the grocery store, and then filled up my sub-compact car with gas at the station there. Spent more on gas than on the groceries. I need to put my car on a diet.

Dear Dewey,

Somehow the topic of my children (specifically my sons) came up in one of my classes today, initiated by one of my female students. I'm pretty sure her real name is Goldilocks because it went something like:

Me: "J.D. is 22"

Goldie: Disappointed look on her face … thinking, "Too old."

Me: "Luke is 21."

Goldie: Same disappointed look.

Me: "And then there's Stephen. He's 15."

Goldie: Grins from ear-to-ear, never raising her sheepish glance up from her desk.

Dear Dewey,

As much as I would like the evenings to be a time of rest, they are usually filled with things I could not do during the day while I was at work. Such was the case today.

My wife is on a litany of medications. Most of these can be ordered online and sent through the mail. One of these, however, can only be picked up at a pharmacy in person—I believe it is a federal law or something. They also will not let me put in the request until there is only a week's worth left. So, last Saturday I dutifully put in my request for this special medication. Of course it needs her doctor's approval first, which I suspected would not happen until Monday. I checked the status on Monday, and then again on Tuesday, only to find out the pharmacy was waiting on the doctor's approval. I sent him an email Tuesday saying he needed to send the approval, as time was running out for me to get the medication by Friday. I checked the status this morning (Wednesday). Still waiting … wait, there it is—but now it only says it is being processed, nothing about it being ready for pick up. I called the number on the bottle (for the second time this week doing so), and jumped through all the automated hoops, only to find out the prescription number had changed, meaning that I could not order any more at this time. I got the pharmacy operator on the line and explained my confusion and frustration. She checked on the prescription … yes, it had gone through, but the closest pharmacy to me (the one we typically use) was all out of the medication and would need to order more. Good for them, but that does not help me NOW. She said she would check a different pharmacy … yep, there was one twice as far from which I could pick it up. She put the request in and said I could pick it up at any time.

We made the drive, and upon arrival I had Chau sit while I waited in line with everyone else. The person at the counter let me know it had not been processed yet, for me to have a seat—it would be ready in 10 minutes or so and they would call my name. We sat and people watched (and looked for our name on "the big board") for 30 minutes. I then got back in line and asked a different person at the counter about the prescription. He checked, could not find it, and asked a supervisor. Apparently it "got lost in the system." He sheepishly said, "Please have a seat. It will be ready in about 10 minutes and we'll call your name." At this point I'm pretty much ready for some medication. Approximately 10 minutes later we were walking out with our one small bottle knowing that we'd get to do this again in 6 weeks or less. Still, better than the DMV.

Dear Dewey

My children have always attended school in a different district than where I teach. Today, one of my daughter's classes spent the period watching the Giants baseball game. Really? I get called into the principal's office if I show a 15 minute documentary on the causes of the American Revolution. Is it too late for me to pursue a new career? (And I do not want any mail from Giants fans claiming the educational and/or social value of watching the Giants.)

My children have come home on other days and told me about a movie they saw in class. It was never to try and get the teacher in trouble, but just a passing comment. As a teacher, I know the value of visual representations of what they have been learning, especially in history. It often helps cement the things they have studied, and we get to discuss what the movie got right, and what was merely Hollywood.

But some of the movies my children have seen in their school seem to have no educational value. I ask them what assignment was associated with the movie. To my dismay, there was no assignment. They just sat and watched it for 90 minutes. Some movies were rated R. Sure, most of the students have seen far worse things at home, in the theaters, or on their phones, but most districts in this area have a board policy that teachers in any of the schools can only show movies with no rating higher than a PG-13, or in some cases, a PG.

There was the one time my son told me what they had been watching. Again, I didn't see the educational value, especially for the class in which it was shown. I asked him about it and he simply said, "Oh, it was a 'free day.' About every other Friday we have a free day and we watch a movie. The teacher sits at her desk and grades papers." Again, as an educator I get that. The grading of papers is a seemingly never ending task. That said, at least show something that is educational. And related to your subject matter. And where most of the actors keep their clothes on.

Dear Dewey,

For the past three to four weeks, I have been covering one of my favorite historical time periods from which to teach—The Industrial Revolution. It holds so much that relates to today, and some shocking elements that arrest the attention of the students.

Throughout this era, there were some major social reforms taking place. Great steps in education. The beginning of the Women's Rights Movement. The Abolitionist Movement. During the lecture today, among these reforms, we discussed the Temperance Movement. I had to take time to explain what temperance is, how serious the alcoholism issue was at the time, and what it mean to be a "teetotaler." As part of my lecture, I presented a picture of an old French poster showing a man drinking absinthe, with an evil looking "Green Fairy" messing with his head.

Always wanting to bring some interesting, practical insight into the lesson, I took a couple of minutes to explain what absinthe is. I explained how it was the popular drink among writers and artists in Paris, that it's called the "Green Fairy" because of its typical pale green color, and how high the alcohol content could be (between 45-75%). I went on to mention that there was a particular ingredient, thujone, that reportedly contributed to hallucinations on the part of the consumer. At that, one of the students blurted out with an excited "Wow!" I never get that kind of response. All eyes being on her, she said unashamedly, "I mean, I wonder what you'd see." This was followed by some mild teasing form the other students. In all honesty, who wouldn't wonder about such things, especially such a young, inquisitive mind as hers? I went on to inform the class that absinthe was banned in numerous countries, including the United States, for over a century. It was only just recently that one could purchase it legally in the U.S., with a few limitations— one being the absence of thujone.

I don't know if the student who got excited about the idea of experiencing a hallucinogen will recall much else from our study of the Industrial Revolution. I do hold out hope that she will not be repulsed at the idea of learning about things in the past. Who knows, some of that old stuff just might make you say, "Wow!"

Dear Dewey,

A few students were in my room discussing Proposition 60 which would require, among other things, that male "adult film stars" wear a condom while filming. A more innocent female student asked, "So is that (requirement) for those in the movie, or those watching the movie?"

You can't make this stuff up, folks.

Dear Dewey,

I teach, among other courses, AP U.S. History. Advance Placement courses are approved by the College Board, and are intended to be college level. Students take the College Board subject test near the end of the school year, and if they pass it, they can earn college credit. Part of my responsibility is not just presenting the material in lecture, but providing them with structure and practice so as to prepare my students for the year-end exam.

One of the ways I prepare my students is to give them practice writing a variety of timed essays that will be similar to those they will encounter on the College Board exam. Recently, I gave my AP US History students a "timed-write" that had a prompt concerning the ratification of the U.S. Constitution. Not only are students required to present an organized formatted essay that is well reasoned, but they need to support their arguments with historical facts. All this is done with what they have stored in their heads; no notes or computers can be used during the writing, and they have 40 minutes to write it.

This particular timed-write came at the end of a long unit on the founding of our nation. The unit included events leading up to the American Revolution, the war itself, through the Articles of Confederation, and ended with the ratification of the Constitution. There were many days of lecture and discussion, but to mix it up and to keep the students from getting bored, we played review games, viewed a documentary or two, and watched two clips from the musical, *1776*.

I sat down last Saturday with my cup of coffee to grade the stack of essays the students had written. Having done this for some time now, I can usually tell in the first paragraph who knows what they are talking about, and who does not. There will be those who shine and demonstrate why they are in a college level class as a junior in high school. Others will simply throw in whatever comes to their remembrance from the unit, and hope that something sticks. Such was the case in Peter's offering. He had a few broad points included in his essay, but for the most part it was just an exercise in rambling. The part that had me choking on my coffee was his inclusion of a Benjamin Franklin quote. The first problem was that the quote had to do with the adoption of the Declaration of Independence, and not the Constitution; approximately thirteen years separated these two. The other issue I had with the quote was that it was from the movie, *1776*, not from any historical document that this student had studied. If students are going to include a quote, they should be certain it relates to the topic at hand, and make sure it is not from a Hollywood movie. The College Board expects a bit more than that, and so do I.

Dear Dewey,

Student A and Student B come into my classroom to eat their lunch.

Student A in a frustrated moment: "I have all C's. ALL C's!"

I chuckle slightly at her intensity.

Student A: "You don't understand, Dr. Shelnutt. A month ago I had straight A's!"

Me: "Straight A's?" (She nods in confirmation) "Huh. That's odd, because when I was in school, all my A's were gay."

Student B shrieks with laughter.

Student A was less amused.

Dear Dewey,

One of our contractual obligations is fifteen hours of adjunct duties. These are hours put in outside of the classroom that are somehow directly related to the students. It might be selling tickets at a sporting event. It could be acting as a sponsor for an on-campus club during lunch. Some chaperone school dances. I have usually fulfilled my hours through coaching Powder Puff football. Many schools have Powder Puff football, and it's simply a single day where the girls play a game of flag football. Ours is a little more intense.

As it stands right now, we have two weeks of practice. It is up to the coaches (two per team) to decide how many practices they run. Most run three or four practices a week, usually for about 90 minutes per practice. I know of one set of coaches that use every bit of those two weeks, electing to practice on the weekends, too. After that, every class team plays every other class team, making for three games, and ending with the championship game involving the two best teams. If you are coaching the seniors, you get the added joy of leading them in a game against the seniors at our cross-town rivals. It's a lot of work, but a lot of fun, too.

Though it can be an extremely frustrating experience, coaching the freshmen or sophomores is a hoot. They are so green and most have no idea what to do. You tell them to run left, and they run right. They will block, but forget to pull flags. Don't even think about using proper terms like wide receiver or running back. Trying to get the quarterback to put her hand on the center's butt would take an act of God. During one game, I told two defenders to stick on the wide receiver like white on rice. The very next play they ran into the backfield, leaving the wide receiver wide open, resulting in a touchdown for the other team. When I pointed out their error to them, one girl simply said, "I didn't know she was going to pass the ball." One of my defenders was good about sticking with the receiver, but when the ball was passed, instead of intercepting it or at least knocking it down, she cringed and hid from the ball. Touchdown!

Not only do they not know what to do, but the new players don't know what to expect. Sure, it is flag football, but they think it is the flag football they play in P.E. It's not. It's much more physical. I have gotten used to the girls, after the first few set of downs in their first game, coming back to the sideline and saying something to the effect of, "That girl hit me in the boob." The first time I heard that I laughed (inside) and simply said, "Well, hit her back." Teaching them how to be aggressive is difficult.

During practice today, we were running through some basic plays. A defender was going for the flags when she grabbed the runner's flag and shorts. The defender pulled with all her might, ripping the shorts right off the runner. Instantly, amidst the laughter, the girls circled the shortless girl as she put on a pair of shorts offered to her by a teammate who happened to have a pair of spandex shorts underneath. This is why we tell the girls on Day #1 to wear spandex shorts under their regular shorts. If someone can rip spandex shorts off you, you have bigger problems than being shortless.

Dear Dewey,

At tonight's Powder Puff game:

Student player: "Doesn't that (crescent moon) look like a toe nail."

Me: "Yes, it does. It's God's toe nail."

Student player: "That's a big toe."

Me: "Well, He's a big God. I don't know about your God, but mine is big." Mutual laughter ensued.

Dear Dewey,

I don't always coach freshmen and sophomores in Powder Puff. Today in practice I was reminded of my first experience so many years ago. I was green, but the girls were not. This was the senior team. They were hard workers and tough girls, but things were not going so well for them. We were in the last game of the Powder Puff season, and we were losing. It's okay to lose if you're a freshman, sophomore, or even junior, but not if you are a senior. The clock was ticking down, and it seemed inevitable that we would lose.

The opposing team had the ball and my girls were trying to keep them from scoring yet again, despite being extremely tired. It was a running play, and it looked like the girl was going to make it around the corner, outrun our defense who missed the flag a few times, and make it into the end zone. Well, one of my seniors wasn't having any of that. Kelly was a big girl, not fat, but strong. Despite being larger, she was very athletic. She was also a country girl, which many of the girls in our community are. Somehow she got into the backfield after the handoff had occurred. She was several yards behind the runner but never gave up. Both came toward our sideline and I could see the sheer determination in Kelly's face. With arms pumping and legs striving, she caught up with the runner. Now, this is where fact and legend get a bit blurred. When Kelly caught up to the runner, many swear she grabbed the other girl's ponytail and pulled her to the ground. Being only a few feet away, I saw her take both her hands, slam them onto the runner's shoulders, and take her to the ground like she was in a rodeo during the steer wrestling. All the male students in the stands gave out a collective grunt. Sure, she drew a penalty flag, she was benched for the rest of the game, and we lost the game, but she showed grit and determination, and will be talked about at future reunions. I wish we could bottle up that determination for our green freshmen and sophomores, minus drawing a penalty flag.

Dear Dewey,

Today, after finding out her test score was higher than she thought it would be, a student exclaimed for all to hear, "Shelnutt, you're the plug!" According to the other students in the class, that's a good thing.

Dear Dewey,

We classroom teachers are like priests or pastors. We do not get to hand pick those with whom we must apply our trade. In our calling, we deal with those who love us and those who despise us. We have individuals who actually look forward to seeing us and our welcoming smile, while others tolerate us and seek to find new ways to undermine what we are doing, despite the fact that we are trying to contribute to their well-being and their wholeness. And like ministers, we have to do this while all the time keeping our composure, never letting the raw side of our humanity show.

Generally speaking, I'm not a yeller. I don't scream at my students, and only once was brought to the point of telling my class to "shut up." (Which, when it happened, you would have thought I'd dropped an F-bomb. Come to think of it, that might have been better received.) Sure, I've used my "teacher voice" to speak over the students to bring them back into focus. I can always tell when I have used my teacher voice because I can feel it in my chest; in my lungs.

Today my students were more than just a bit out of control. They weren't mean spirited or anything, just overly excited to see each other. Usually getting them under control is like herding cats, but today it was more like herding honey badgers, which, incidentally, are said to "emasculate" larger animals for no apparent reason. Two students in particular were laughing and chatting about, despite my repeated request for them to refocus and become a part of the class. Clearly, I was dead to them. Frustrated, but with a calm, firm voice, I was going to send them with a referral to the "time out" room on campus when I elected to allow them to carry on their conversation out in the hallway. They reluctantly, and a bit bitterly, went out.

After the two left, another student who had a look of concern on her face said, "Your face kinda got red." Still riled but keeping my composure, I looked coldly at the student and assured her, "Oh, you haven't begun to see the shades of red I can turn." Not my best moment, but I left the campus today under my own power and without a police escort.

Dear Dewey,

In high school and college I was introduced to the thrill of performing in comedy sketches. This lead to a television show on the local access station with some of my college buddies. I've always been a performer at heart. For me, that's one of the draws of the teaching profession; it's like "Open Mic Night" every day. When it's Spirit Week, I do my best to dress in accordance with the theme of the week/day. Of course, Halloween is one of my favorites. This year I was a grave digger, with a body wrapped in a blanket and ready for burial. I've dressed as Frankenstein's Monster, a zombie, half man / half woman, a Vegas swinger, and even a serial killer who dressed like a little girl and carried around a creepy doll. My all-time favorite was a deranged clown. I walked into one freshmen English class and brought one of the girls to tears. You really don't get that sense of accomplishment until you make a freshman girl cry.

November

Education is the passport to the future, for tomorrow belongs to those

who prepare for it today.

– Malcolm X

Dear Dewey,

With the encouragement from my students and friends (mainly on social media) I "campaigned for president" in the last election. Here is an actual text communication from this morning with one of my constituents, my wife Chau.

Me; "Happy Election Day!"

Chau: "I'll vote for you."

Me: "You already did."

Chau: "Was I drunk?"

Time to start gearing up for the next election.

Dear Dewey,

I just realized that "multisyllabic" is a self-defining, self-illustrating, and self-promoting word. Words are fun. Sometimes they are misleading or confusing—like "jumbo shrimp." Other times words need context to help you determine what meaning is to be attached to them. At the beginning of a school year, I'll often do an exercise with my students to illustrate this very point. I have them divide a piece of paper into four sections. "In section #1," I tell them, "draw a picture of a 'trunk.'" I instruct them not to discuss it, and that they will not be graded on their artistic ability. After a minute or two, I tell them, "In section #2, draw a picture of a 'trunk.'" This, I say, must be a different "trunk" than the first. Not a different version, but a completely different type. After another two minutes, I say, "In section #3, draw yet another picture of a different type of 'trunk.'" At this point, there is some giggling and looking at each other's papers. "You likely can see where we are going with this. Draw a fourth picture of a 'trunk' in section #4." Most will get two or three different pictures, but only a handful will get four. Then I show sample photos of a trunk and ask

76

who drew a picture of what is shown in the picture. They normally don't realize how many there are (i.e. elephant trunk, car trunk, travel trunk, tree trunk, swim trunk, trunk of the body, and the slang usage of trunk to refer to one's butt).

This is a fun exercise and gets them thinking. We talk about how they would know which trunk someone is talking about. If I say, "Don't get too close to the trunk" they still don't know what I am talking about. Then I ask, "What do I need to know?" The students will say more information, or a greater context. I explain that these are the kind of skills needed in understanding the past. If nothing else, we get to have some fun with words. Eat your heart out, English Department. Sorry, Math Department.

Dear Dewey,

Student A: "Dr. Shelnutt, is it true that you were a model?"

Me: "Define 'model'."

Student B: "Underwear model."

Student C: "I could see you as a game show host."

(Somewhere in the 90 minutes we learn something about the Industrial Revolution and World History.)

Dear Dewey,

Sometimes when my students are self-correcting their work to multiple choice questions (where the choices are A, B, C, D, or E), I will clarify the answers by things like "B as in boy," "D as in dog" and so forth since some of these letters sound similar. For fun, I will often pick a theme and have them come up with an appropriate answer (i.e. if the theme is breakfast cereals, "C as in Captain Crunch"), and the rule is no repeats. Today's theme: places in the U.S. ("B as in Boston," "A as in Arizona"). As we had gone through about 25 questions and the students were competing to see who could come up with the next response, I said, "C as in ..." A student blurted out immediately, "Kansas." We all had a good laugh, and the offending student took it all in good stride.

Dear Dewey,

I love teaching about the Industrial Revolution. One gets the feeling that he is at the start of the modern era. The machines making textiles, trains going 20 mph, canal boats with flat bottoms ... That reminds me, there was this girl I dated back in high school ... but I digress.

Dear Dewey,

Me addressing my students: "I can prove that dogs are better than cats. Whenever you see a homeless person, what do you see with them? It's always a dog, not a cat."

A student's hand immediately shoots up, straining to be seen.

Me continuing: "Unless, of course, it's one of those crazy cat ladies ... but she, by definition, is crazy."

Hand drops back down to the student's side.

Dear Dewey,

When I get the opportunity to teach Government, it affords me the chance to engage the students in some honest debate, more so than my other classes. My favorite time to teach this subject is during an election cycle, especially a presidential election. All I have to do is listen to talk radio in the morning, or watch the news the night before, and the "hot button" topics are clearly revealed. Some of the students will even have heard something about these issues, and many are forming an opinion about them. At the beginning of the course, and reiterated throughout, I let the students know that we will be discussing some controversial topics, and that everyone should feel free to voice their opinion. I tell them I'm not looking to sway them to my way of thinking (I usually try to stay neutral but will ask them questions to see if they have really thought it out and can defend their position). I do insist, however, that though they might not agree with a fellow classmate, they must always be respectful.

I believe it was my first time teaching Government when Proposition 8 was put before the voters in California. If passed, it would have made a marriage between a man and woman the only valid and recognized marriage in the state of California. It passed, but was later struck down by a federal court. Prior to voting day, my classes discussed the proposition in open debate. This was not a formal debate by any means and anyone could offer their position and insight. My requirements were the same as always: you must respect each other's right to have and express an opinion, and when giving your position, you must support it thoughtfully and reasonably.

I'm sure there were a number of students who shared, but only two still have a place in my memory. The first, and I believe the first to speak, was a young man who was in favor of the proposition. From what I recall, he gave some of the basic reasons you would expect to hear from one opposing same-sex marriage. Then he punctuated it by ending with the words, "And remember, God created Adam and Eve, not Adam and Steve." While this drew a few chuckles and high fives from his buddies, bumper sticker political rhetoric does not go far in a debate setting.

The other student who took a place behind the lectern to voice her view was one of the young ladies in the class. She was one of my sharper students and had a wry wit that could cut through hardened steel. As she began her delivery, her voice quivered, but her authenticity never faltered. She spoke of how she was bi-sexual and that many of her friends were gay or bi. She expressed how she did not see how a couple in a loving relationship could possibly hurt others, even those who did not agree with their choice. She made her case and returned to her seat. There were no other volunteers that period.

My recounting of this debate is not to bring attention to Prop 8 or the issues around it. Nor have I any desire to share my own personal convictions concerning same-sex marriage. But the brief interchange brought to my mind some of the highs and lows of debate in society. As I write this entry, the current political climate in the country is not a healthy one. Having become so partisan a civilized discussion can't really occur regarding what is best for the country and society. The "Adam and Steve" sound bites rule the day, and the one who can yell the loudest is given the 30 second clip on the evening news. Whatever became of the reasoned, maturely delivered expression of thought? I fear it may have been left back in that senior Government class so many years ago. Tell me your convictions through a shaking voice. I might not agree with you in the end, but I will listen to you.

Dear Dewey,

Back to school/work tomorrow (including an after school-day meeting). Time for the 3 week crunch before finals. Sorry, kids, I don't offer extra credit (see the class syllabus). I was asked by another teacher how I felt about late work. I told her she knew how I felt about late work. Here is the equation as I see it: Late work + Unexcused Absence = Spawn of Satan.

Dear Dewey,

Today in AP World the class discussion centered around various island chains. I have heard that no man is an island, but what about an isthmus? Can a man be an isthmus? (If he can, I've got dibs on the Isthmus of Kra.)

Dear Dewey.

Student: "You know, Dr. Shelnutt, your sarcastic voice and your normal voice sound very close, and it's hard to tell them apart."

Me: "Oh, really?"

Student: "Yeah, just like that."

Dear Dewey,

When I was a young lad, my family had the privilege to travel via airplanes quite a bit. Since we flew stand-by, we didn't always get to sit together. As we disembarked from one particular flight, the older woman who had been sitting next to me for six hours leaned over and told my mother, "He sure does like to talk." In some social group settings this may not be the case or seem obvious, but put me in front of a group to speak and you can't shut me up.

The truth is, I love to tell stories. So it is that I find myself as both a high school teacher and a church preacher. Both afford me the opportunity to spread my storytelling wings. I suppose the story telling is merely a vehicle that brings me to my greatest delight—bringing laughter to others. Not just the simple surface laughter of a knock-knock joke, but genuine, heartfelt, do-your-soul-good laughter. While I think the ability to do such a thing is either a part of one's DNA or it isn't, to refine it as a skill takes tutelage.

As I look back at those who have shaped me most in both my love for storytelling and for laughter, three men stand out: my father, my life-long buddy John, and Thom, my spiritual father. These men have been indispensable as friends and mentors, even if, per chance, they won't claim me. I do not pretend to even come close to the fringes of their craft and skill, but they have been prodding me along the way. While I have either lost or broken most of the gifts given to me over the years, the gifts of story and laughter will remain with me to my final breath. When one dear friend once wrote to me, "You make me laugh," I told her, "I'd be happy with that on my gravestone, 'HE MADE US LAUGH'." I'm still good with that.

Dear Dewey,

I just heard that the Canadian Immigration website has crashed after the most recent election. Seems people on both sides of the political aisle have made the threat that if their candidate did not win the election, they would move to Canada. Folks, we are a democratic republic. Every four years, there will be those who are pleased with the outcome, and just as many who are not. To say, "That's it, I'm outta here" (like many Republicans did when Pres. Obama was elected) is reminiscent of the kid at the playground who said, "Well, if we're not going to do it my way, I'm taking my ball and going home." I would hope that we as a nation are better than that. For over 200 years, accepting the outcome of an election, and there being a peaceful change of leadership, has been the hallmark of our society and the envy of many nations (and their citizens) around the world.

Dear Dewey,

My wife and I were out picking up a few items after I got home from work. We decided to spoil ourselves and dine at Panda Express. After the meal had been enthusiastically consumed, we cracked open our fortune cookies. Chau's said something about living a long and joyful life with your partner. Having heard such a positive forecast from hers, I ripped into mine with unabated anticipation. My words of wisdom and hope for the future were, "A vigorous hike and fresh air are just what you need." I don't know about you, but I don't need my glorified fast-food eatery to remind me that I am fat and in desperate need of exercise. I've got a large mirror at home that gladly communicates that to me on a daily basis. (Besides, have you seen that panda? He's not exactly ready for the Olympic Time Trials.)

Dear Dewey,

Went with my wife, Chau, to the hospital pharmacy after work to pick up a prescription refill for her. We decided since we already made the drive, we'd swing by the Flu Clinic for our flu shots. Finally, something that lives up to all the hype! It's only been two hours and already I'm feeling fluish. And they were handing this stuff out for free like it was candy on Halloween night. God bless America. Then again, this year is shaping up to be one of the most challenging in my teaching career. Maybe it's just my body dealing with residual, pent-up frustration that I've tried to suppress throughout the day.

Dear Dewey,

Like any profession, education has a language all its own. Such terms like depth of knowledge, learning targets, growth mindset, small learning communities, IEP, 504, walkthroughs, and SWBAT are all too familiar. There are others that are not as technical but just as frequently used. One such term is "helicopter parent."

A helicopter parent, as the term implies, is a father or mother (often both) who is not only involved in their son's or daughter's education, but pushes them beyond what would be considered normative or healthy. Think of a little league dad or stage mom, only in the academic field, hoping to live vicariously through their child's future at an Ivy League school.

As an Advanced Placement teacher, I have had more than my share of these parents. Sure, the initial communication with them is pleasant enough, but if they don't get the response or action they desire, things can escalate quickly. See, these guardians aren't like your run of the mill "Eye-in-the-Sky" traffic helicopter. Oh no! They are more like an Apache Longbow swooping in for a full frontal attack.

Earlier in my career, I had a student in one of my AP history classes who had been absent for a timed-write exam. This is when they are given a prompt on which they are to write a fully devolved essay on the spot. The College Board does not tell the students in advance what the prompt topic will be, but I do so that they can develop their writing skills. I don't tell them the exact prompt, but I do tell them the general topic or era. In this instance, the prompt was going to address the Industrial Revolution.

The student was making up the exam during the class period while I continued to work with the other students. He was placed at the back of a row to give him a space a little more conducive to writing. As the period drew to a close, so did his time to complete the exam. I looked over to check-in on him, only to notice that he was looking at his cell phone, hidden under his desk as it rested on his lap. Students are not permitted to have phones out during class time, and certainly not while testing. I approached the student, took his test, and mentioned that it was unfortunate that he made the choice to use his phone as it would result in a zero for his exam. At the bell, he left without comment.

An hour later I called his mother during my prep period to explain the unfortunate occurrence. The mother told me she knew of the events earlier that morning as her son had already called and told her. Then the mother shot off her first missile by letting me know how disappointed she was in me—how as a professional I should have taken the time to find out why her son had his phone out (even as the mother acknowledged that it was against school policy to have it out). I explained it didn't matter, even if it was to check what time it was, because if the student had his phone out during the College Board exam, he would be kicked out of the exam, and put the exams of every other student in jeopardy.

The mom swung back around for another shot. She informed me that the son had found a great quote when he was studying for the exam and he wanted to get it just right. Sounds noble enough, but it still is not permitted. I then explained to the mother that what the son was writing down was not simply a quote from some great historical figure, but rather the first paragraph from the entry on the Industrial Revolution found at Wikipedia; verbatim with no credit given or source cited. I further explained that this was called plagiarism, and not only would he be kicked out of a College Board exam for such a practice, but could be kicked out of university for it. There was a long pause as she hovered. Then she slowly backed away saying, "I guess we'll just have to agree to disagree." While I should be flattered that she would think I am the one who is re-defining the criteria for what constitutes plagiarism, I'm pretty sure it's well established.

Just yesterday another copter, I believe this one was a Blackhawk, came knocking on my door. This had nothing to do with an exam, but a unit assignment. For every chapter I provide students with about fifty questions that they are to answer as they read the chapter. These questions are based off a test bank that the publisher created for teachers. I use the test bank to create my unit exams. Unfortunately, someone across this great nation of ours decided to upload all the answers from the test bank onto a popular online study site. Knowing this, I tell my students that they are to use their books, and their books alone, to answer the questions. If I discover they have used this online site, even for one question, they will receive a zero for the assignment. Since the test bank uses unique wording not found in the book, it is pretty easy to find those who take the short cut.

The first time through, about half the students challenged me on this. Zeroes were given and continued warnings proclaimed for the next few unit assignments. Still, they did not believe I would find out. More zeroes.

Enter the Blackhawk. Most parents show up with a cordial demeanor—at least for the first three minutes or so. Not this father. He was red-faced before I could even get my classroom door unlocked. After reassuring me that he supported my practice of giving a zero for students who cheated by copying from the online site, and that his son deserved the first zero, he quickly turned against me. The father said he checked on his son throughout the night and saw him with his book. The father, I was told, even turned off the internet connection. There was no possible way that HIS son could have cheated. I showed him one of the answers in question (one of the more obvious ones). He reiterated that his son had not cheated. I gave him a copy of the textbook, opened to the appropriate page, and told him to show me where his son got the answer. He scoffed and said he didn't have time to read the chapter. No worries—as the answer was found in the paragraph to which I was pointing. "I don't care what you say, but I know my son didn't cheat. You are just a lazy teacher." I'm not sure where that came from, but we moved on.

I'm pretty sure he would have hit me at some point had his wife not been there. She did not say much, but I do not think she would have lied under oath for her husband if it came to that. I made him a deal. If his son could show me in the text book where he got his answer, I'd give him full credit for the assignment. He repeated what I said, almost in disbelief that I was such a reasonable individual. He assured me his son would do just that the following day.

Today the young man did come to me, book and assignment in hand. He opened the book and showed me the appropriate paragraph. To his dismay, I pointed out I could see where he had erased his original answer, the one from the online site, and written in a new answer derived from the book. At the same time, I showed him the photocopy of his original work that I had made before I had returned the assignment to him. Caught in yet another lie what was he to do? He started crying. Through the tears I heard an apology. I told him that he would be getting the original zero, he had better start doing his own work, and that he needed to go back and tell his father what he had done, and that Dr. Shelnutt was right all along. He told me he would. I should check with the father to see if the son follows-up as I asked, but at this point it just feels vindictive.

Sitting here typing this entry, I wonder if the tears were due to being caught, because he was genuinely sorrowful for lying again, or because he was fearful of his father. Maybe the tears were caused by a combination of all three. My own tears fall at times because of what I see these helicopter parents doing to their sons and daughters. Deep down I think they mean well. How I wish they could see how just a little grace sprinkled on their hyper-involvement would go a long way. Is it worth gaining a Stanford graduate if it means losing your child in the process? If it means giving them a bleeding ulcer by the age of 14? What will this mean for their grandchildren? Will the sins of the father be visited on the son?

December

Develop a passion for learning. If you do, you will never cease to

grow.

– Anthony J. D'Angelo

Dear Dewey,

Overheard during passing period, as students were coming out of their last period class: "It's things like that that make you want to go kill someone." I'm pretty sure they were coming out of a math class.

Dear Dewey,

Language fascinates me, and I often use word play with my students. One of my favorite parts would be idioms. Even in the same language, time and space can change what may seem common place. For instance, what were Grammar Nazis called before 1920? Grammar Huns? Grammar Mongols? Grammar Aztecs?

Dear Dewey,

It is inevitable that when I get a new batch of students, those who have never had me as a teacher in previous years, the topic of my age will come up. Sometimes it surrounds my birthday, others are just random times; at least random from my vantage point. So it was that today a student bravely raised her hand and asked how old I was.

I never tell students outright how old I am. Not that I care they know, nor am I one who frets over getting older, but I enjoy hearing their answers when I ask, "How old do you *think* I am." Let me tell you, they are never shy about offering their reasoned answer. It usually starts in the mid to upper thirties. When I scoff at such an answer, I can count on the next answer being in the low forties. At the writing of this entry, I am in my low(er) fifties. My students' gross underestimations are not due to me looking exceptionally young for my age, nor is it due to them wanting to be overly kind. Part of it is because to them, anything over thirty five is old, so their answers reflect that. The other main reason for the obvious mistakes is that a majority of fourteen and fifteen year olds have no concept of time. To them, their first decade and a half felt like an eternity.

Herein lies one of the struggles of teaching history to anyone under the age of thirty. Let's face it, most of us did not like history when we were in our K-12 education. Sure, there are exceptions (I was one of them), but 99% who find out I teach history will respond apologetically, "Uh, I didn't really like history in school." That's okay. I didn't like diagraming sentences when I was in junior high, and now … nope, still don't. Trying to get adolescents who can't see past three inches in front of their faces and their own world to have a global perspective that reaches down through the ages is asking a lot of the students, and the teacher. The good news is, more adults than not will grow in their appreciation for things past.

So high school students are terrible at guessing the age of an adult. They're not missing out on much—except, perhaps, getting a job at the carnival midway.

Dear Dewey,

Happened upon "The Spy Who Loved Me" on TV. What a dreadful movie. Awful writing and even worse acting. The film became enjoyable when I imagined Adam West (of the campy "Batman" fame) taking the place of Roger Moore (who, in my opinion, was the worst James Bond). Now THAT would have been a movie!

Dear Dewey,

Did some work in the backyard today. Cleared out weeds and what little grass I have to prep for some landscape rock. Eventually had to take the weed whacker to it. Should have picked up the dog poop first. Weed whackers and dog poop don't mix.

Dear Dewey,

While at the grocery store this evening I found myself in the dairy section. There in front of me were two rambunctious children running amuck while their tired, young mother scouted the variety of creamers. Dodging the little rascals, I opened the glass door and bent down to grab a gallon of milk from the bottom shelf. Feeling inspired, I made a quick barking sound and looked at my wife saying with mild shock, "There's a dog in there." We walked toward the bakery, peering over our shoulders at two wide-eyed munchkins searching for the dog in the refrigerated section. Yep, I'm pretty proud of myself

Dear Dewey,

When I started at this school site over ten years ago, I realized straightaway not to count on the majority of my regular education students to do much of their assigned homework. I recall my first day I instructed the students, who were juniors, to read the next section in their textbooks for homework, and be ready to discuss the content the next day. This amounted to three pages of reading (with pictures, no less). I had a student literally laugh out loud. The thought of simply reading three pages was beyond conceivable for him. True to their expectations, none of the students did the reading. From that point on, I decided to make the vast majority of their work due at the end of each class period.

During today's class, we read together three excerpts from the Industrial Revolution that related to child labor. These were primary source documents. We had some class discussion about the various views represented in these selections. The students had some good insights and contributed appropriately, so I decided to give the class an assignment that would require them to do some work at home.

The assignment was to write a letter to a factory owner as if they were a child working in one of the workhouses of that era. There were some specifics to which the students would have to abide, such as margins, font size, and length, but at only three-quarters of a page long, and simply using their imagination, it would be fairly brief. Finally, they would have to "cut-and-paste" a picture from the internet onto their letter representing what they had written. Though they should be able to do this in an evening, I gave the students a week to complete the task.

As my third class of the day was about to start, the first student strolled in and laid her backpack down at her desk. "I heard about our project."

At first I was a bit confused. "Project?" I asked.

"Yeah, I heard about the project we are going to have to do."

Oh, the one-page letter. As she didn't have the details yet, I assured her that one would not characterize it as a project. After all, a project usually requires some type of research, multiple drafts to work through, and takes weeks to complete. Projects require special material. In elementary school, you know it's a project if it involves things like Popsicle sticks, clay, or colorful pipe cleaners. In middle and high school, it's not a project if it doesn't include a trifold poster board. I challenged her to wait until the end of class and see if it's really a project.

When class was over, she raised her hand. I called on her as the other students were packing up to leave. With a smile of resignation she said, "Yep, it's a project." I respectfully disagreed. Either way, it's due next Wednesday at the start of class.

Dear Dewey,

I just received a text letting me know that the school and the surrounding areas are under a tornado warning—that we should seek shelter immediately. Because the threat of wildfires, earthquakes, mudslides, and flooding aren't enough.

Dear Dewey,

I'll say this about the flu, it makes for a great weight loss program. Sure, like all fad diets, I'll gain all the weight back, and then some. For now, feelin' the burn!

Dear Dewey,

Today I had a sub cover my classes. About the only time I do that is when we, the staff, have some kind of Professional Development training that I am required to attend. This time, though, it was due to illness. I was feeling overly fluish yesterday during class and put lesson plans together in case I got worse.

I really don't like getting a sub. My wife tells me all the time I should get a sub and take a "mental health" day off. There is some validity to such days. The thing she doesn't understand is that it is twice the work to have a sub for just a day; that it stresses me out all the more. I have to make sure it is a lesson that anyone can do, as rarely do you get a sub that has a degree in my course matter. It should be something that will keep the students busy for 50 minutes (or 90 on a block schedule), something that can be completed within that time, and something the students can do with little to no direction or help. Then there is the issue of class management. I know that I will likely have to address discipline issues from the day I was out. Finally, despite the best laid plans, it appears some subs simply do not read the notes I left them, or they simply disregard them.

Now, I am not down on subs and the service they provide. I started my public education career as a sub in a very difficult district. There were days I drove home from a day of subbing thinking, "No human being should be treated like that." I was young with only two years of private school education experience under my belt. I was called almost every day, making $70 per day. Today, they do everything via computers, but back then you got a call. I'd wake up minutes before 6:15 a.m., waiting for the phone to ring. They would ask if I wanted to sub at a particular school, and would tell me what I would be teaching. This didn't matter too much as (1) you usually taught a subject you were not equipped to teach (such as the time I taught French for three days), and (2) you might agree to one job, but be reassigned when you got there. This second point always irked me. Being young and foolish, I tried to dress professionally. For me that meant a tie and more times than not, a sports coat. I looked like I was running for president of the local chapter of the Young Republicans. I would get there looking like a fresh-faced stock broker, only to be told that I'd be covering P.E. instead. There were, of course, those days that I would be called to cover a P.E. class, showing up in a warm-up suit, only to be directed to the math department. Either way, it paid $70, no benefits.

There were always discipline issues, but it could just as well be the adults that made your life hard. For one assignment, I showed up at the designated high school, signed in, got the keys, and made my way to the first period classroom. I was subbing for one of those teachers that moved throughout the day; a total of three times. I went to the classroom and looked everywhere for the telltale sign—a manila folder. None was to be found. I went back to the main office, thinking perhaps the teacher had left it there. Nothing. I got a hold of the textbook, and with some direction from the students as to what chapter they were on, I had them do my world-famous review game. As the students left at the end of the period, one said, "I learned more today than I have all year." I finished out the day doing the same thing every period. When I got to the last class of the day, in the last classroom of the day, low and behold, the lesson plans for the day. Why would an educated person think I would look in the last classroom for the lesson plans? Maybe they were in a hurry. Or just lazy. Thanks for nothing. Still, $70.

The one subbing assignment that will forever be engrained in my mind was the time I was called to the district's "alternative" school. These were for high school students who, usually for behavioral reasons, couldn't hack it in the mainstream school. There I went, all banker-like. Good news was I was teaching History, my forte. Bad news was, I was also covering P.E. Seems this teacher was the social science/P.E./boys basketball coach juggernaut. Being the dutiful substitute, I sought to follow his instructions to the letter. For P.E. I was to get the group of boys into two teams, and have them play a round of basketball. Seems a few of the older, larger boys wanted to run the show, and leave the younger, smaller boys out. They said they had an upcoming game for which they needed to practice. The latter group didn't have a problem with that. Didn't they understand … there was a lesson plan to be followed? I attempted to regain order by getting the one and only ball from the ring-leader. Instead, they thought the lesson plan called for "keep the ball away from the lame substitute." I hate that game. I figured there was no reason to be the monkey in the middle and went to get the principal. As we walked out to the outdoor court, I explained the situation. He called the ring leader over and asked what was going on. He told the principal about the upcoming game. The principal thanked him and told him to go back with the other students. It was at this point that the principal let me know the lay of the land. He amended the lesson plan and instructed me, "As long as they aren't hurting each other, just let them do what they want." He then went back to his office, leaving me without a single ounce of authority with those students. That was my first experience at that school. I never accepted another assignment there. You can keep your $70. I'll sleep in.

Dear Dewey,

I went to Burger King to dine this evening (don't judge me). As I walked up to the young man behind the counter to place my order he said, "Hold on just a sec. My register has locked up. When I have too much money, it won't let me do anything." I immediately replied, "Sounds a lot like my wife." Well, at least *he* laughed.

Dear Dewey,

This morning I had a first in my class. Actually, a first for any class I have taught. After completing his test and reading a book while other students completed their test, a student had a seizure. I did not notice it at first. I had bent down to answer a question of another student when a student said somewhat calmly, "Dr. Shelnutt." Almost immediately, three more students joined in, but with a greater sense of urgency. I thought maybe someone had come into the room and the students were trying to make their appearance known to me. When I looked up, I saw what was going on.

Since my wife has seizures, I was fairly well adept at aiding the student. As I kept the student safe from self-injury, I turned to another student and told him to go get security. As the student headed out on his mission, I noticed that though the seizure seemed to be subsiding, the student's body emptied his bladder. I told the rest of the class that they needed to get up, and quietly go outside to the courtyard, and wait for me there. As they did, security came, the student regained consciousness, and he was attended to by the school nurse. I rejoined my class outside. We went to the library so that one of the janitors could get the room cleaned and sanitized.

It was a difficult, and a bit awkward, situation for everyone. The students, however, were amazing. They were helpful, did not take advantage of the situation by roaming the campus when I sent them out of the room (yes, some would do that), and kept their heads about them. And despite what I thought would occur, I did not hear murmurings throughout the day from other students about the morning's events. Not bad for a bunch of squirrelly high schoolers.

Dear Dewey,

There is an old adage that says that girls mature faster than boys. Now, some will say that is all it is, an old saying, without any weight to it. Yet I believe most can see that, physically, girls mature faster than boys. A visit to any middle school will bear this out. Girls tend to be taller, and often stronger, than their male counterparts. Perhaps the adage was also referring to emotional or social maturity, and it is this to which people object.

Let me present People's Exhibit #1. In a lecture on the Early Industrial Revolution, I instructed how the Agricultural Revolution was an initial cause. One of the advancements during this time in England was the control of water and usable farming land through earthen dams. When I mention, and it is shown on the screen, that these were known as dikes, without fail a number of the boys will grin and look at a buddy across the room. I've been teaching this class for over ten years and never ... NEVER ... have I had a girl do the same with a female friend. I do not acknowledge the boys' obvious juvenile behavior, but perhaps I should. I usually hurriedly say that we do not often use this term, but in California we talk about levees. This is something they know about, and we can have a halfway intelligent discussion of the usefulness of levees.

People's Exhibit #2. When I am letting students know how they did on a test, I give them the option of me calling out their score, or coming up and seeing it privately. On occasion, they will have me call out the grade they earned and the score is 69. I started teaching in 1986, and not once did I have a girl get that score and her female buddy from across the room say something like, "I know you like it that way." I wish I could say the same about the boys.

Having pled my case for the old saying, there are exceptions to the rule, thank God. I have seen more than my share of fine young men who are respectful, mature, and thoughtful beyond their years.

Dear Dewey,

Scene: First day of Christmas Break; in the kitchen getting breakfast.

My wife, Chau, takes down a bowl and her every-morning container of Fruit Loops from the cupboard. Our beagle, Zack, begins to jump wildly, like a 19 year old boy on his first Spring Break to Miami when the Hawaiian Tropic Sunscreen bus pulls up. Now, I never give Zack "human food." Makes me wonder what goes on in this house when I'm at work.

Dear Dewey,

Although a product of the 70's, I had never seen a single episode of CHiPs—that is until recently. Having no cable, our choice of channels is limited. One such choice is a local station which airs reruns of CHiPs. Based on the two episodes that I have seen, all the women driving the freeways of California in the late 70's were blonde and bra-less. Who knew?

Dear Dewey,

After clearing the cobwebs in my head with a cup of coffee, I decided it was time to clear the ones in our sun room. It was so bad it looked like a scene from an old Vincent Price movie. Having done the job, I grabbed my second cup of coffee, ready to sit and do some reading and studying. It was about that time I felt something crawling on the back of my neck. Yep, I had picked up a passenger. Sure, I was able to smoosh the little sucker in my hand, but still not a feeling I care to repeat anytime soon.

January

A person who won't read has no advantage over one who can't read.

– Mark Twain

Dear Dewey,

I'd like to dedicate this next song to a love from which I must part.

Christmas Break, this has got to be the saddest day of my life

I called you here today, Christmas Break, for a bit of bad news

I won't be able to see you anymore

Because of my obligations, and the ties that you have

We've been meeting here every day for 2 weeks

And since this is our last day together

I wanna hold you just one more time

When you turn and walk away, don't look back

I wanna remember you just like this

Let's just kiss and say goodbye

(The obvious homage to the Manhattan's song duly noted)

Dear Dewey,

Well, another "first day back" is behind me. It's January, but at the start of the second semester I often get a whole new set of students for a semester-long class. You never really know what to expect. First impressions are not always correct, and each class will take on a personality of its own—and likely change over the school year.

Among my many new students is a highly functioning autistic student. I have had such students in the past. Almost always they are quite a pleasure to have in class. Sure, some of the social skills and filters might be lacking, but they more than make up for it in other ways. This specific student seems to be quite intelligent, but falling a bit short in the social graces.

While explaining the key points of the syllabus, Tammy raised her hand and drew all of our attention to the question of cheating and plagiarism. This is mentioned in my syllabus (which is what caught her eye), but I had not yet brought it up with my students. "I see here you speak of cheating and plagiarism. What if I read a book or essay by an author, and was inspired by what they wrote, so I wrote an essay on the same subject, but in my own words. Would that be plagiarism?" The other students started looking at each other, wondering what was going on. I assured the student that I would not consider that cheating in any way. "So being inspired by another writer is okay?" I underscored to Tammy that being moved by the writings of others is at the heart of education.

Later, I had the students respond to three brief questions about themselves, their goals, and what they feel about history. Soon, the bell rang indicating the end of class. Tammy waited until all the other students had left the classroom before approaching me at my desk. "I wanted to talk to you personally about what I wrote; face-to-face. I believe you are a good teacher. You are enthusiastic about your subject matter, but ... I don't think I want to be in the class any longer." I asked why, so she continued. "I just don't want to waste my time. I think it is a waste of my time, and your time, for me to be in here. I want to take a class that will further my career goals. Again, I think you are probably a good teacher because of your enthusiasm. I wish you could be my physics teacher." I shook her hand, gave a word of thanks, and redirected her concerns to an academic counselor. Tammy needs my class to graduate, so I fully expect to see her tomorrow.

Never a dull moment.

Dear Dewey,

During the past semester I had a male student in my 6th period class who, right after lunch, had come late to class virtually every day. Not extremely late, but about five minutes late. Apparently, he was smooching on his girlfriend until the bell rang, presumably outside her 6th period classroom, which made him late. However, with us being three days into the new semester, I noticed he had been on time every day. As I was passing back some work, I jokingly said, "Hey, I notice you've been on time every day this week. What happened? Did you break-up with your girlfriend?" With a forced smile, he simply mumbled, "We're kinda on a break right now." Crud, it just got real. Sorry, my man, I didn't mean to call you out like that.

Teen drama ... I can't say I miss it.

Dear Dewey,

Wow! What a stellar weekend. Well, stellar up to that point when I was pulled over for "exceeding the posted speed limit." On the bright side, based on the officer's claim, my speedometer seems to be accurately calibrated.

Dear Dewey,

Historically, my afternoon classes tend to be my most challenging. The students are amped up on all the sugar and carbs they digested at lunch, and I'm beat and quickly running out of energy. On top of that, many of my more "challenging" students are given double math and English classes in the morning to help them along, which means concentrating them all in my afternoon classes. This year is no different. As it stands, my 5th period and 7th period classes are competing with one another for the title, "Most Obnoxious Class." Seventh period is beginning to pull out in front, but never discount the efforts of 5th period.

I look at the progress of my 7th period class, the last class of the day, and it's not looking so good. Last semester, the class average was a full 20% lower than my highest achieving class. I've spoken very calmly, but frankly, already this year about both their academic and their behavioral progress. There was a moment in the class today where I felt we needed to have a Come-to-Jesus talk. I tried to explain that for some of the students, they needed to make the conscious decision to begin to move from being a child to a young adult. I have many fine students, including some in my 5th and 7th period classes, but many of them act as though they are still in the 3rd grade. (If I wanted to teach elementary age students, I would have signed on for that. These are folks who will soon be eligible to vote for our next president. Now there's a sobering thought.) I emphasized with my students that they are old enough now, and have been doing this student gig for at least ten years now, it's nothing new—and that they are the ones who have to take responsibility for their own actions and their own learning. I firmly, yet without raising my voice, told the class that I would likely see some of them this summer (i.e. in my summer school class). One of the students busted out with an "Ooooooh," as a feigned expression of being scared. I assured him that I wasn't trying to threaten anyone, but that after 23 years in education, I know how this will play out if they continue to make the choices they are making.

During this same class period, a female student near the back, who doesn't speak up all that often, raised her hand and asked if I had recently gotten a haircut. I acknowledged that I had, and she simply said, "It looks good." Almost immediately there came, from various points throughout the classroom, despairing remarks; not about my hair but about her saying it looked nice. I could see she was almost sorry she had said a word. I quickly tried to redeem the moment and make it a teachable occasion. I thanked her for noticing and for the compliment. I then asked the class what was wrong with giving a compliment.

What have we become as a society if you can't compliment others without the fear of some kind of reprisal? I try to model this with my students on a regular basis. It might be a new hair style or color of hair, a shirt or shoes that really stand out; maybe a time when a student shows some school spirit by dressing up for one of our Spirit Days.

As I drove home, tired as usual, I thought back over my 7th period class, and other instances from the day. I do not believe I am asking too much from my students, or that I have unrealistic expectations, but many of my students are just not there yet. Some of it is their intellect and lack of academic success from the past, but much of it is simply maturity. Sure, kids will be kids, but I have noticed the gradual decline of maturity of my students over the years. Generally speaking, they are academically about the same as my students have been over the years, but the recent students have excelled in their immaturity. They are not at the place I would hope they would be. As I drove home considering these things, I thought, "Isn't that what education is all about?" The point at all stages of education is not to just appreciate where they are currently at, but to move them forward. They are to be compelled, whether they know it or desire it, to be brought along to greater maturity—both intellectually and socially.

What are the two things needed to transform a piece of coal into a diamond? Time and pressure. I only have a limited amount of time with my students, so I must be ready to keep that loving, yet unyielding, pressure on them.

Dear Dewey,

I just found out that the line in CCR's "Lookin' Out My Back Door" isn't "Look at all the happy preachers dancing on the lawn" but rather, "Look at all the happy creatures dancing on the lawn." Suddenly, my whole life feels like a lie. Next thing you're going to tell me is that the line in the same song, "Mammaries and elephants are playin' in the band" is also wrong.

Dear Dewey,

It's Monday morning and quite early. I typically get on campus before the other staff and faculty members. I like to get ahead of the traffic on my 45 mile drive, and to get ready for the day with planning and correcting assignments. This morning I am reflecting on the events of the last 24 hours. It was not the weekend I had planned.

Yesterday, Sunday, my wife, son, daughter, and I traveled two hours to the wedding of the son of close friends of ours. It was great to see some familiar, if not a bit older, faces. The reception was a time of celebration. There was fantastic food, music, and loads of dancing; the latter of which I was a spectator. I don't dance. With the hour getting late and a two hour drive still ahead of us, I rounded up my two youngest children and my wife and loaded them into my Corolla for the drive. Just as we got our seat belts locked in, Chau started making that low level groan indicating she was entering into a seizure. We've seen hundreds of these since the onset of her illness, though they seem to be increasing in frequency and intensity. There's not much for us to do other than make sure she is safe, and let her ride it to the end.

Sure enough, less than five minutes later she has come out on the other side. By now we are on the freeway. Traffic is relatively light for this part of the Bay Area. We slow down only long enough to pay the bridge toll. Next stop should be home, a mere 90 miles away. The classic rock station is playing on the radio and the hum of the tires is trying to drown out the music. Suddenly, I hear a beeping sound, like my car was going to self-destruct in five seconds. I'm looking at my dash board to figure out what is going on. As I do a new sound, that of whooshing wind, joins the symphony of noise. It's at this point that I realize my wife had taken off her seat belt (the beeping sound) and was about to step out of the car—which is going 70 miles per hour at the moment. I reach over and close her door. "What are you doing?!" She calmly informs me, "I need to go use the restroom." I assure her that we will pull over at the next stop and find one for her. The rest of the drive home, all I could think about was what would have happened if I hadn't acted fast enough.

Why did she do this? A development in her illness, associated with her seizures, is that when the seizure subsides, she can enter into a time similar to that of a sleep walker. She appears awake, but is in a world of her own. The first time this happened, I had just come home from work and was in the kitchen preparing dinner. She was hit by a seizure, which was followed up with her dropping her pants and sitting on the kitchen trash can. She thought she was in the bathroom. What is a husband to do? I let her finish.

Now here I sit, in a classroom that will soon be filled with 35 high schoolers full of life and attitude. This emptying and filling will be repeated another four times throughout the day. In each class I have to be "on." (The way I teach requires a lot of energy.) As I tell folks, most days are like open mic night in my classroom, with the exception that I am the sole performer. Five shows a day, five days a week. ("Try the meatloaf. Remember to tip your waitress.") And, for the most part, teachers do what they do in isolation. I've had a couple "teacher homies" through the years, but most of them have left for other school districts. That's another story for a different day.

So I sit here on a Monday morning, still a bit numb, wondering how I will teach World War I effectively today. And where will my wife try to urinate today? When she first became ill, we hired someone to be with her during the day. That was a disaster. On top of that, I can't afford to hire anyone. We do not owe money to anyone, except the mortgage. We do not live beyond our means. We haven't even been on anything that even looks like a vacation in over ten years. We pay our bills, but it is pretty much pay check to pay check. So, hiring someone to help out when I'm not home simply is not an option.

Some have asked, "Well, can't she get some disability or something?" We applied for that when she first became ill. The official we met with said that she had not worked enough quarters to qualify. See, my wife made the choice to rear and nurture our four incredible children as a stay-at-home mother. He informed us that if she could get in five more quarters, she would qualify. I could not believe that actually came out of his mouth. I looked at him with what I can only imagine appeared as ice cold eyes and explained to him, "But - she - can't - work! That's why we're here." He sheepishly replied, "Yeah ... that is a problem."

The events of last night remind me that we all have struggles and pains that we carry, that few, if any, know about. That includes my students. I hope my difficulties help make me a more empathetic and compassionate teacher.

Dear Dewey,

Just got back from the follow-up endodontist appointment for my root canal. At one point the doctor used what I am pretty sure was a hot glue gun. Time to think about upgrading the dental insurance.

Dear Dewey,

Famous Quotes:

"Get off my lawn!"

- Walt Kowalski (Clint Eastwood, *Gran Torino*)

- Me (5 minutes ago)

Dear Dewey,

I have not kept it a secret that this year has shaped up to be one of my more difficult ones. I primarily have sophomores this year, and they certainly are living up to the reputation they gained as freshmen. They are, as a group, one of the most disrespectful, rude, loud, disruptive classes I have ever encountered, and I've encountered quite a few. It is funny how a class can gain such a reputation, and it usually starts to build while they are in middle school.

So it was, at the end of this particularly hard day, as I was sitting at my desk questioning my career choice, that in walked a former student who had graduated a short time back. She was on campus to help her sister out with some things when she decided to swing by and say, "What's up, Doc?" Seeing Lisa's broad smile brought back a flood of memories associated with her and her siblings. Lisa is from a large family. In fact, I had Lisa and three of her siblings in my classes over the years. I started working at the school too late to have some of her oldest family members as my students. Though each of the four that were in my classroom had their own distinct personality, each to a person was a joy to have. I was at three of their graduations, with one more to come. I have attended graduation parties in their backyard. I have received verbal and written words of encouragement and affirmation from these siblings and their parents.

This fleeting, precious moment with Lisa reminded me of why I show up at 6:20 a.m. every morning, knowing that someone during the day is going to yell at me, "Fuck you," and some of those will even be students.

Dear Dewey,

I drive about 45 miles one-way to my school. The freeways around the greater Sacramento area can get pretty congested, so I have made it a habit to get an early start, usually getting on the road by 5:40 a.m. or so. This puts me on campus around 6:20 a.m., giving me some time to prepare for the day. Even at this early hour, all kinds of things can happen on the road. Who knew so many people were up that early?

One morning while driving my usual route, I began to merge over to make my connection from one freeway to another. This is the midway point of my commute. As I switched lanes, I saw an object begin bouncing directly toward me. It appeared to have dropped from under the car in front of me. I had no time to respond without putting other drivers at risk, so my car took the full brunt of the hit. Pulling

over to the side, I got out and examined my car. The front bumper had

sustained some damage and the bouncing object was now wedged

under my car. It was a tire. I was going to jack my car up but decided

to try and "un-wedge" it. Getting back into my car, I put it in reverse

and hit the gas pedal hard. After a quick surge backwards, I was free

from the rogue tire. Not how I wanted to begin my day. Repairs would

be made and Ol' Blue would be around for many more miles.

On this particular morning, I entered the first of three freeways

that I travel. At one point it goes from two lanes to three, adding a

merging lane to the right. I was in what became the middle lane when I

suddenly had two trucks on steroids on either side of me. You know

the type—the ones that make you wonder what the owner is

compensating for and require one of those airplane mobile staircases to

enter. Well, I suspected something bad was about to happen when the

monstrosity on my left decided to take my lane. No blinker; no

warning. I blew my horn, stepped on my brake, and turned my steering

wheel all in one coordinated move. Suddenly I found myself spinning across two lanes as if I was in a Keystone Cops movie. When my car came to a stop the two trucks were long gone and I was on the shoulder facing the wrong direction. Another driver sped past, flashing his lights and honking at me. I sat there with my heart pounding in my chest and said out loud, "God, why do you hate me so much?" I'm pretty sure He had a good chuckle over that one.

February

The highest result of education is tolerance.

– Helen Keller

Dear Dewey,

Got home from attending Day 1 of my first ever Social Studies Conference. Some pretty good workshops. I attended a breakout session that focused on the Vietnam War. I arrived early so I could find a seat on the aisle near the back. A tall, older gentleman came in late and sat right next to me. Apparently Fred is a heavy breather. It was distracting, but I figured I'd get used to the wheezing after a while. The workshop speaker asked questions of the attendees, and a few people spoke up (seems we had a few veterans in the audience who contributed much to the discussion). Fred answered, too, but only loud enough for me to hear. I think I would have been okay with this, but I swear he sounded like Powers Boothe recounting how he made it across the DMZ undetected in the middle of the night in a rain storm.

Looking forward to Day 2.

Dear Dewey,

Day 2 of the Social Studies Conference (as of this morning): (1) Two

insightful presentations—one dealing with using graphic (historical)

novels to get students interested in history and reading, and the other

looking at how we can teach diverse world religions in general and

Judaism in particular; (2) I scored 15 more free pens from

vendors/publishers; (3) A "Meet Mark Twain" event at one vendor,

which I'm pretty sure was just Mr. Herbert from The Simpson's with a

white wig and fake mustache; and (4) an older gentleman thanking me

in the lobby for the question I asked at a workshop—however, I have

yet to ask a question in a workshop (clearly, he could tell just by

looking at me of the bounty of insightful questions I was pondering).

Dear Dewey,

The label "entitled" is often attached to the current younger generation. The idea that "everyone gets a trophy" definitely seems to bear some truth. Clearly, it is not an obsolete label. I've witnessed this attitude in both the regular school year and in summer school. Many students will come to class, be totally disengaged, do none of the assignments, fail every test, and still try to reason with me that they deserve a passing grade. I remind them that the class is called "World History" and not "Attendance." They're not getting units toward graduation just for showing up.

Talking about entitlement is a bit tricky because of the demographics my school serves. Many of these students come from very impoverished households. A majority of our students qualify for free or reduced cost lunches. Some of my students rarely see their parents because mom and dad leave for work before their children get up for school, and get home late in the evening. They are lucky if there is any food in the cupboards at home, let alone any mid-morning snack in their backpack. I'm actually sympathetic to the plight of my students. I keep some granola bars and cup-a-soups in my cabinet for students who do not have anything. A number of students eat their lunch in my classroom. Several times I have seen a student sitting at a desk, texting on their phone or school-provided tablet. I ask if they have anything for lunch. Usually it is met with a simple, "No." I'll ask if they want a soup, or maybe a hotdog (which I often eat). Sometimes they accept, other times they do not. But their response is always different from what I was hearing today.

Today's evidence of entitlement is a bit trickier. I had an unusual number of students ask me, both in my classroom and in the hallway, if I had any food. All of them, to the student, asked in the same way. Not in a thoughtful, somewhat humble, reaching out sort of manner, but rather like I was the public pantry to which they can swing by and get the goods anytime they want. All petitioners asked with a tone of expectation and with a smidgen of demand. In a word, entitled. Some students asked if I had any water. I reminded them of the numerous water fountains on campus, including the one 20 steps from my door. The reply was always the same, "I don't want *that* water."

If nothing else, these dilemmas bring to mind that most people in our community, and in our society at large, have no idea what takes place in our centers of education. It is far more than "reading, and writing, and arithmetic." It is about teaching, yes. But it is also about nurturing, loving, and in many cases feeding, our youth. I am the first to say that the public school, the government, is not to take the place of the parent. In far too many cases the parents have abdicated their responsibility to the school. Entitled? Perhaps. But sometimes, they're just hungry.

Dear Dewey,

This week at our school we are having another "Spirit Week." This week's theme is "Reality TV." Today is "What Not to Wear" day, so I did my best job mis-matching every aspect of my outfit. No one seemed to notice. Should I be concerned?

Dear Dewey,

While previewing a movie this evening in preparation for upcoming classes I saw a number of trailers. One was apparently rated PG-13 for, and I quote, "violent content, brief strong language and smoking (historical)." Historical smoking? What, pray tell, is "historical smoking"? Did they smoke so differently in the past that it needs to be noted in a movie rating? "Put the kids to bed, there's going to be some historical smoking." Really?

Dear Dewey,

From time to time I have my students watch documentaries on topics we are covering. I try to select ones they will find insightful and at least moderately interesting. There are other times I select a Hollywood film that reflects time periods we have recently discussed. Not only do I want these to be interesting, but I usually select films that the students have not seen, and ones for which they would not select themselves.

So it was that today I had my students view Charlie Chaplin's *Modern Times*. I teasingly tell the students that not only is it in black and white (eyes roll) but it is a silent film (groans). The film isn't completely silent, as there is music, sound effects, and a few points where there is talking, but as the last major American film to use dialog cards, it is a silent film. I show it to expose them to a great piece of film, one they would never likely see otherwise, but most importantly, because it shows one view of the concerns of industrialization on the individual and society. Without fail, most of the students will enjoy it more than they thought they would, and more than they are willing to admit.

When I have students watch a film they do not just sit there passively taking in the sights and sounds. I almost always will give them a "Viewing Guide" which will have a series of questions to which they are to respond. This assignment will be due immediately after the film is done. As I sat at my desk at the end of the day grading their work, one paper stood out more than the others. Most of the responses were fairly typical and what I would expect from high school sophomores. As I came to one student's work, at the very top left of the paper where I had typed "Name: _____" for the students to write their names, this student wrote "Modern Times." If this was the first Viewing Guide that the students had ever done for me, I might understand. Or if it was the first worksheet I had ever had them complete, perhaps. But they are in their tenth year of formal education; certainly this was not the first time this particular student has had to write in his name at the appropriate place. It would have made a little more sense if he had written his name somewhere else on the paper, but he didn't. So, from this day forward, I will refer to him as Modern Times, or M.T. for short.

Dear Dewey,

Started the work day with a student (senior) bringing in a half-dead rat (not a pet) into class. The student could not understand why I had a problem with this. Later during a "black out" rally, a different student (also a senior ... no connection) pelted me several times in the back with various items. Thankful for the upcoming three day weekend. Oh, wait ... I've got a potential root canal on Monday. Bring the rat back.

Dear Dewey,

Last week, to illustrate a point during a class discussion, I borrowed from a quote by Abraham Lincoln and asked my students, "How many legs does a dog have if you call his tail a leg?" After a moment of thinking the students answered in virtual unison, "Five." We live in society where objective truth is disappearing and subjectivity reigns. I love my students (I believe they know that) and love the opportunity to challenge them to think through why they believe what they believe. (For those of you reading this who also answered, "Five," to Lincoln's question—the correct answer is "four." Saying that a tail is a leg does not make it a leg.)

Dear Dewey,

This morning I was just launching into one of my lectures when my vision began to spin. I've had vertigo attacks before, but I don't recall having any in class. I paused for a second thinking it would simply wash over me as it typically does. Unfortunately, it intensified to the point that I was finding it hard not to fall to the floor. I was able to make my way to my lectern and use it for support. I told my students in my best calming voice, "I'm having a little vertigo episode right now. It should pass in just a second." Students stared; eyes widened. "If for some reason I end up on the floor, I would appreciate it if someone could go get security." Eyes widen even more. Silence. Finally one of the students broke the silence saying, "You're putting a lot of pressure on us, Dr. Shelnutt." So much for having my back.

Dear Dewey,

I visited the public library today on a whim. It has been years. Decided to check out five DVDs. The mild-mannered librarian informed me that I owed more than $20 for an overdue bluegrass collection CD from 2015 (something you could find at Goodwill for $3). She deleted the charges. I'm pretty sure the fact I was checking out the original "Shaft" had a lot to do with it. Shaft ... he's a bad mother (shut your mouth). She must have thought I was B.A., too.

Dear Dewey,

Got to my classroom at 6:15 a.m. The temperature in the room was a comfortable 73 degrees. The HVAC system kicked on at 6:45 a.m. I had the thermostat turned all the way up to 90 degrees. By 7:15 am the room was at a cool 67 degrees. That's one way to keep the students awake.

Truth be known, our system is very outdated and does not work as it should. It's so old, you can no longer get parts for it. If it fails and needs new parts, they have to be special ordered and machined, costing the district thousands of dollars. Right now there is a measure on the ballot for the folks in the community to decide if they want to allow for a bond to be issued to get a new HVAC system at the school.

It won't be cheap. One individual during an open forum on the bond

measure made a comment along the lines that she didn't think this was

a need, but rather a want. I'd like this individual to come to my

windowless classroom on a hot day when the temperature inside

reaches 86 degrees. Then, this same individual can try to keep 35

squirrelly sophomores interested and engaged in learning about the

Ottoman Empire. Then tell me it's merely a want. I double dog dare

you.

Dear Dewey,

Today's scuttlebutt on campus, unbeknownst to most of us teachers,

was the rumor that a student in attendance had a knife. No knife was

found. Personally, I have never felt concerned that a student would

pull a knife on me. And because of the agricultural roots in this

community, I could see why a student might carry a pocket knife with them. Still, a "Zero Tolerance" stance when it comes to weapons or potential weapons is a good thing.

Just this morning I heard on the news of a middle school student in Georgia stabbing his teaching in the chest (the teacher survived). At this point, they have not given details as to what prompted the student to stab the teacher. Did the student bring the knife to school for the purpose of injuring the teacher or others? Did the student get upset and simply react in the moment; a crime of passion, so to speak? These are the things teachers across the country deal with on a daily basis; at least the potential for such things.

In the same news report I heard of a woman who, due to her overhearing a conversation and diligence, thwarted a potential mass killing at a high school. It seems to me that shootings and stabbings are on the rise. Did these things happen with the same frequency when I was going to school, or is it just reported over more media instruments than before? I'm sure there is data somewhere to tell us. It is not as easy as just saying, "We need greater gun control." I believe it is a greater societal issue; an issue of the human heart. And simply declaring it a "Zero Tolerance Zone" will not stop these horrific events. Our school is also "Zero Tolerance Zone" for drugs, and you can just imagine how well that has turned out.

Dear Dewey,

It was one of those long block days. Classes are 90 minutes. On this particular day I started the class with some extended lecture. The students were surprisingly patient and kind to let me get through 45 minutes of material. I'm not saying they were hanging on my every word, but they were not disruptive. After I was done waxing on eloquently, the students had a writing assignment they were to work on in response to my lecture.

Just as students were getting started, Jack approached me at my lectern as I was gathering up my notes. Jack is, sadly, one of those text book loners. He is bigger than the typical boy his age, a bit out of shape, and never says a word in class. He sits by himself in the front row and never interacts with the other students. I've sought to reach out to Jack, but with little success.

As Jack drew closer, I simply asked, "What can I do for you, sir?" In a very steady, nonchalant voice Jack asks, "Can I step outside and put my eye back in?" With that he opened his hand to reveal a glass eye. "Of course." (What else could I say?)

Maybe I missed that day in my credentialing program, but I don't recall them telling us what we are supposed to do when a student's eye falls out.

Dear Dewey,

I was digging through some boxes in the garage trying to find an old gadget. As I dug to the bottom, I found a small innocuous yet colorful book. There was no title on the cover, so I opened it to see what it was. Turns out I had rediscovered an "autograph book" I used back in my third year of teaching; from twenty five years or so ago. It was from my first full-time, public school position. I was too cheap to buy one of the end-of-the-year yearbooks, so I bought this hardcover half-sized notebook to have students write year-end thoughts to me. It was completely voluntary on their part, but from what I could see, many chose to write something.

There were two things that struck me as I read the various entries. First, the students wrote with reasonable eloquence. To put it in perspective, these were junior high students in a fairly impoverished town. Most comments were kind, some humorous, but all contained complete, grammatically correct thoughts and varied vocabulary. The other striking element was the handwriting; it was spectacularly wonderful. I could actually read it. Sure, some of the writing excelled and were not just legible but beautiful, but none of the remembrances looked like they had been written by a 98 year old who had been shot and was about to die in the next thirty seconds, and he wanted to send his loved ones a final message with his last breath.

Why the dramatic difference in writing and handwriting between then and now? When I tell my students they need to answer in complete sentences, you would have thought I had asked them to give me one of their small organs. When I look at what they turned in, I have to wonder if they even know what a complete sentence is. Just because it has a lot of words does not mean it is a complete sentence. As for handwriting, one would think either we offer a course in hieroglyphics or that there has been a moving of the Holy Spirit and the students are writing in an ecstatic language.

Is technology to blame? Have today's students lost their ability to spell due to spell-check, or to construct a proper sentence due to grammar help from our computer programs? Maybe it's the cell phones that have taught students how to text in code. I hate to blame the ills of education and of a generation on technology as if I was a Luddite, but when Patricia turns in an assignment and has written her name as "P@," a few red flags go up for me.

Dear Dewey,

I have to imagine that as long as there have been school desks, and students to sit at those desks, there has been writing on desks. I don't get that. Even when I was in school, I would see where students who shared my space in other periods drew on the top of the desk. Now, I liked doodling just as much as the next kid, but I had paper bag-covered text books and Pee-Chee folders on which to write.

So it is that at least once I week I will walk up and down the rows of desks to check and clean up any desk that has writing on it. Truly, there are generational differences. When I was a kid, we were creative. Our writing might take the form of some witty comment, but more times than not, it was some goofy cartoon, or for those who felt a bit more bold, it involved crude drawings of erogenous zones. My students aren't so imaginative. Other than the occasional gang tag, I mostly get scribbles. That's it—scribbles. Just lines going back and forth. On particularly longer days, a student might get the entire upper corner of the desk drawn in.

Teachers have several common, reoccurring daydreams. One is where we tell the parent of an underperforming student just what we really think of little Billy, but we refrain in reality because want to keep our jobs. My fantasy is to go to the home of one of my desk-artists, sit on the couch and scribble on the living room coffee table. If the student invited me over for dinner, I might take out a pencil, or even better, a permanent marker, and doodle geometric shapes on his kitchen table. Who knows, maybe I will feel bold enough to draw something a smidgen more provocative. After all, what could he do, give me an hour detention?

Dear Dewey

March

To educate a man in mind and not in morals is to educate a menace to

society.

– Theodore Roosevelt

Dear Dewey,

I went to donate at the blood drive at our school today. An attendant said I couldn't because I'm just getting over a cold. I walked to the other table to be screened as a bone marrow donor. That interviewer said I was too old. I haven't felt this rejected since that dance back in junior high.

Dear Dewey,

Every once in a while, folks from the District Office, the community, or visiting dignitaries stop by our campus and check-out what we are doing in our classrooms. Sometimes, I'll let my students in on the visit and enlist their help in a little fun. I instruct them that when our visitors come into my room, I will ask my students some review questions; those who know the answer are to raise their right hand, and those who don't are to raise their left hand. I tell them I will only call on those with their right hand up. If only left hands are up, I'll say something like, "Wow! You all know that one. Let's move on to the next question." This gives the appearance that all the students are well informed and that I'm an amazing teacher. I will let the guests in on our little fun before they leave the classroom.

Well, today was such a visit. I informed my class of the impending visit. They seemed to accept it with great eagerness and smiles. Sure enough, ten minutes later our visitors were at the door. After inviting them to have a seat, I continued my lecture. The time was ripe. I said, "Let me pause for just a moment. My students are eager to show you just how much they know." I put forth a "softball" question for them to fully connect with and hit it out of the park. It was material we had just gone over five minutes earlier. This was going to be my finest moment. The question was posed; not a single hand. Not one. Finally, after repeating the question, two hands went half-way up. At least they were right hands. I posed a second question, emphasizing how EVERYONE can participate. A few more hands went up this time, but only about six out of a class of twenty-seven. I felt I had to explain to the visitors why I was pounding my head on the lectern.

I've never been so disappointed. Time to retire and open that bait shop I've always dreamed about.

Dear Dewey,

We are officially halfway through the second semester. Usually by now, my class roster is pretty well settled. All the shuffling that goes on during the first three weeks or so has ceased. Not so this year. I have received four new students over the past two weeks. These aren't students who have had their schedules changed, which is normal, but rather students who are new to our school.

Yesterday's addition, Miguel, just arrived from Mexico. Again, nothing terribly unusual about that. We have many students who have come from Mexico, or who have family there. I offered the student a class syllabus in his choice of either English or Spanish – he replied, "en Español." I then informed him as to where to sit, since I use a seating chart. He just sat in the closest seat. I once again redirected him. He looked puzzled. A student next to his assigned seat tapped on it, and the new student moved there.

Later on in the day I received an email from a staff member letting me know that I'd be getting this new student, along with information regarding the credits he would be getting for the class. I e-mailed back an inquiry as to his grasp of the English language. The reply was, "Very little." It was suggested that I sit Miguel near a Spanish speaking student. I did just that today. I first asked some of the young men who was sitting next to him, but none spoke Spanish fluently. I asked one of my female students, Cassandra, who was entering the classroom if she spoke Spanish. She said she did. "Fluently?" I asked. She said she did. I explained the situation and asked if she would be willing to have him sit in front of her, and she could help him get acclimated to the class. She said she would.

Miguel came late to class today, escorted to the classroom by one of our EL (English Learners) specialists. I directed him to the seat in front of Cassandra. What I observed next, while it wasn't earth shattering, completely gave me renewed hope in this generation. As Miguel sheepishly made his way to his seat, Cassandra stood up, extended her hand, and introduced herself to him. I had not asked her to do that, but was thrilled that she was mature and caring enough to initiate this kind act. Miguel was able to be engaged in the lesson, and completed the assignment, albeit in Spanish. When class was over, and the students stood to exit, Casandra again extended her hand and shook Miguel's hand. They were talking about something as they both left for the day.

I'm not sure how successful Miguel will be in the class, but if more students showed as much thoughtfulness as Cassandra demonstrated today, our world would be moving in a much better direction.

Dear Dewey,

Students never cease to surprise me. At times for the better; other times, not so much. I've heard some of the most compassionate, caring utterances come from my students' mouths. I've also heard some of the shallowest, self-serving blatherings, too. Still other times, I just sit there and wonder what their lives are like outside of the classroom that has caused them to respond in such a disassociated manner. One of these moments came within a month of arriving here. It occurred many years ago, but it came to my mind this afternoon on my drive home.

I began this job mid-year, at the start of the second semester, my third time being in this situation. It's hard enough starting at a new place where you have no reputation among the students, but starting mid-year ramps that up a few notches.

A month into this new gig, my wife and I went away for the evening. Our church youth group was going to use our house for an all-nighter. The girls were to stay at one house, while the boys stayed at ours. Seemed going away for the night would give us a sound sleep.

The day after we got back, Chau was feeling fluish. She had just started a new job, but ended up staying home and in bed the entire week. Every time I called to check in on her, I woke her up. That Friday, when I got home, she was in bed asleep. I fed our kids and watched a movie with them, checking in on my love from time to time—each time she was asleep. When I finally decided to call it a night, I got cleaned up and went to bed. As soon as I was under the blankets, Chau sat up, but she did not respond to my questions about how she was feeling. Nothing. After seeing that her eyes were open, but she was not responding in any way, shape, or form, I took her to the E.R.

Fast-forward thirty-six hours later. The attending doctor asserted she had taken too much of a flu medicine, and once it worked its way through her system, she would be fine. I looked at my bride, who at this point was gnawing at the stitches of her bed sheets trying to undo them, and thought, "It can't be that simple." I wanted to believe him, but I broke down in tears.

The next day, Monday, was a federal holiday, so I didn't have to be at work. As I sat by Chau's bedside, a neurologist came in. He spoke directly to me, as my wife was still in a world of her own. As I suspected, the flu medicine had nothing to do with her current state— she had viral encephalitis. The doctor let me know that Chau had contracted a common virus which typically is dealt with by the body's normal defenses, often resembling a flu. In Chau's case, it went to her head—literally. The brain had been swelling and, if had been left further unattended, could have killed her. The doctors were able to reverse the effects, but the affected part of her brain now had shrunk. Only time would tell how much of her brain function she would regain; we'd have to wait and see how much the brain re-wires itself.

When I returned to the classroom the following week, with students I had only known for a relatively short time, I told them what had occurred. I guess I expected a few "wows" and "I hope she gets better," and indeed there were those. But the first response that I heard came from one of my senior girls who asked, "Are you going to leave her?" To be honest, I was taken back by the question. I looked at the student and could see she wasn't trying to be funny or startling. It was an honest question. Without condemning, I asked, "What kind of man would I be if I left my wife when she needed me most?" I continued on, "Although marriage can be difficult for all involved, the whole 'for better or for worse, in sickness and in health' had to mean something." She nodded in agreement and said nothing else.

To this day, I wonder what provoked such a question. Had she seen a marriage that lacked such commitment between husband and wife? Was marriage just a more legal form of dating, where one leaves when the partner no longer suits you? Did she ever find that someone for whom she would stick with, regardless of how hard life hits—because God knows, it's going to hit, and hit hard.

Dear Dewey,

Last Sunday while at church, I sneezed out loud in the middle of the service. Not a single "Bless you" was offered. What?! I get more than that in the frozen food section at the Super WalMart. Time to find another church.

Dear Dewey,

Today our school experienced another power outage. Apparently it wasn't just our school, but about half the town as well. This may seem like a small matter, but there is one architectural feature of our classrooms that make this quite the event. See, our school was built with no windows. Sure, the main office, library, and cafeteria have windows, but not the classrooms. When the lights go out, you can't see your hand in front of your face, let alone the 35 students in the cramped room.

I remember the first time a black-out happened. As soon as the power was lost and the lights went out, students screamed like they had been attacked by the monster that hides under their bed. I opened the door to try and let some light in, but the only available light comes from the glass doors down the end of the long hallway that leads out of our wing. It's hard enough being in our tiny rooms with that many bodies, but you can imagine the chaos of that same room in complete darkness. Think of how cockroaches scatter when the light is turned on, only in reverse.

Office personnel started their hurried survey of the situation, making contact with the District Office. For some reason, students think there is some kind of Ed Code or law that says if the lights don't come on after 30 minutes, they get to go home. Kind of like being in college, and if the professor isn't there ten minutes after the start of class, class is canceled. The reality is, the powers-that-be at the D.O. have to make that call. And from what I can surmise, they aren't going to even consider dismissing the students until twelve noon. The word on the street is, noon is the magic time in which a district can count the day as a completed school day. Most schools here on the Left Coast don't have "snow days" built into the calendar, so every day is important. My first experience with a power outage resulted with the students being sent home—after a 3 hour wait.

Fortunately for me, the power went out today during my prep period. When the lights went out, I headed to the library for part of the period. Since the library has one whole side that is nothing but windows, I was able to get some grading done. I also visited a few classrooms to check-in on my colleagues, giving them any updates to which I was privy. I will say this for the students—they were, for the most part, orderly. No screaming (at this point), and everyone pretty much sitting in darkened rooms. I account this more to the fact they all had tablets and cell phones from which they could keep themselves entertained rather than their profound maturity. As I walked by each classroom, it was like seeing fireflies on a summer evening.

Students were given an early, and then extended, lunch period. Power eventually was restored and the afternoon classes resumed. All-in-all, not a bad day.

Dear Dewey,

I have been called sarcastic, incorrigible, stoical, smart-ass, and stand-offish, to name just a few. Well, at least I'm not boring.

Dear Dewey,

Every once in a while, I share a story from the headlines with my students. I try to select ones that I believe will spark their interest, and give us an issue to discuss. This past Monday was no exception. I recounted an item I had heard about in a neighboring city. This city is poverty stricken and known as a high crime area. It seems that a business owner had his warehouse broken into several times, with various items stolen. The article related how he was grilling some steaks behind his place of business one weekend when, after going inside for a minute to grab something, he returned to find the grill—steaks, burning coals and all—gone. Apparently that was the last straw for this local entrepreneur. As he left for a short vacation one weekend, he booby-trapped the few entrances to the warehouse with triggered shotguns. After completing the set-up, he had second

thoughts, and disarmed the entrances—but forgot one. As luck would

have it, thieves broke in again, entering at the lone armed entrance,

killing one of the would-be criminals. The story ended by saying the

business owner would be charged with the death of the thief. We

discussed the craziness of the story, if the owner should have a right to

defend his property with deadly force, and if he should be charge with

a crime. I do all I can to stay neutral in such discussions, allowing each

student the freedom and safety to present their reasoned position, but I

did close the discussion with a simple, "It's getting so that you can't

even protect your own property anymore."

Today, three days after the class discussion, I was called into

one of the vice principals' office. He had received a heated call from

the father of one of my students. The VP asked if I had told my

students that they could not legally own a gun, and if I was criticizing

gun ownership. Here I was thinking I was in trouble or that I had done

something wrong. Me? Against gun ownership? Me, who has been

accused of being Ronald Reagan's and Charlton Heston's ideological

love-child? I think I actually let out a laugh. I told my VP that I had
not said any such thing, was not against gun ownership, personally
owned five guns, and invited the unknown father to come look at them
at my home if he wasn't convinced.

It made me wonder what other things I have said, according to
my students.

Dear Dewey,

Yesterday tragedy struck when one of my colleagues passed away. He
had a family and was taken too soon. Today our school community did
what we could to care for our students and one another. As the day
wrapped up, our principal invited all staff to finish the day off in the
library so we could check-in with each other. She asked what we
needed at that time. I thought through my day, working through in my
mind lesson plans, an up-coming professional development, and other
teacher things. Nope, I was good.

In the quiet stillness of my 45 minute drive home, alone with my thoughts, it struck me—what I needed, really needed, was an embrace, a simple hug. Not a virtual one (as sweet as those can be), but a real, person-to-person, wrap-your-arms-around-and-squeeze kind of hug. To envelope, and be enveloped, in the genuine care of another. It was a desire to know that I am a part of our common humanity. The kind of incarnational presence that says we are here for the other, and they are here for us—it's going to be okay.

So, if you find yourself in a similar situation, as we all will at some point, perhaps this little post will come to mind. If it does, reach out and embrace another. Don't let go too soon. There is no substitute for the human touch. Nothing.

Dear Dewey,

Recently, our small town got a genuine fast food restaurant. After months of waiting, our very own Taco Bell opened. While some of the local folks made jokes and complained about the service they received,

I found it to be clean, the workers always greeted me with a smile, and my order was always spot-on. This evening my wife and I decided to dine there, having come off a long and tiring day. As we sat and chatted about how our day went, I read the following on my receipt:

NOW HIRING

Dreams do come true

Now, I worked for 14 months at a fast food burger joint when I was in high school and into my first few months at college. That was about 13 months longer than I thought I'd be there. Looking back, it was a great experience. I tell my students that minimum wage and fast food types of jobs were designed for them. It gives them some spending money, lets them learn how to budget, and helps them to develop job skills (working with others, showing up on time, following the directions of a boss, interacting with the public, etc.). All that said, I don't know that I would say my 14 months was a "dream come true." Still, it's little moments like this that make you ask yourself, "Am I living the

Dear Dewey

dream? Did I follow my calling? Did I turn right on the path to a career when I should have turned left, or kept going straight?" If life has shown me anything, the journey has many ups and downs, dips and curves. If you spend life wondering, "Did I make the right choice, or did I miss 'the dream'?", you will end up standing in the middle of the road, paralyzed from making any movement, and you're likely to get run over. So, get moving. Today's dream might just be a daydream, or a cat-nap. And that's okay.

April

Learning is not attained by chance, it must be sought for with ardor and diligence.

– Abigail Adams

Dear Dewey,

I utilize a variety of games in my classes. I've been using one game that I created since I started teaching back in 1986. It's a mix, of sorts, of *Jeopardy*, *Wheel of Fortune*, and Hangman. I use it primarily with students the day before a test. The game questions are based on the questions on the unit exam. The students typically enjoy it, and can become quite competitive since the winning team gets 5% added to their test score.

I also have games I use simply to build camaraderie among the students. One such game is based off the old television gameshow, *Password*. For the uninitiated, *Password* was a game where contestants give one word clues to get their partner to guess the

171

"password." I've used this as a review game (using terms/people/events from the unit), but at other times, I use the "Home Version" of *Password*. I believe I might have the original 1964 edition that I found at Goodwill for $1.99.

Well, Dewey, today I introduced the Password game to my students. Since we are about half-way through our current unit, I decided to stay with the words that come with the boxed home version. I made sure to choose words that the students would know so they would have a fighting chance of giving decent clues. What is the old saying about the best laid plans?

In one round, the word was "worm." While one student gave reasonable clues to his team, the opposing student gave what can only be described as odd or unique. Clues like, "above" and "high." When the other team won, the student protested, saying "worm" wasn't the password. I assured him it was and showed him. Apparently, he wasn't listening when I said the password would be in the little "red window." Instead of looking there, he looked at the card that slides into the holder, which for simplicity sake says "TOP" at the top of the card so you know which end to put into the holder.

Later in the morning there were two girls who had volunteered to come up and sit in the "contestant" seats, providing clues they hoped their respective teams would get. For these two the password was "fort." I showed them the word and asked if they were ready for the round. One said she wasn't, as she didn't know what the word was. I showed her again. Nope, still didn't know it. I whispered it in her ear. That didn't help. Both the other student and I found it difficult to believe that this 15 year old high school sophomore didn't know what "fort" meant. I mean, we live no more than 30 minutes from Sutter's Fort which every fourth grader in Northern California is obliged to visit on a field trip. Various "forts" are discussed in the curriculum throughout the years. None of that mattered—she didn't know what it was. I selected a different word for the pair and moved on.

In the next class, the password was "bad." The first student gave the clue, "detention." Humorous, and fitting for a high school student to say, but not likely to get the desired response. The next student was ready to deliver his clue, certain that it was a winner. "Brussel Sprouts." First, the points for that round went to the other team because he gave a two-word clue. But I was laughing so hard I could barely write the points on the board. That was nothing compared to the ostracizing he received when his team heard that the password was "bad." Still, he'll live to play another day.

In the last class I had two female friends as opponents. The word was "ugly." One of the girls gave as a clue the word, "Me." She didn't win the round, and I was nearly brought to tears. "Ugly" is how she viewed herself? She wasn't likely to find herself on the cover of the Sports Illustrated Swimsuit Edition, but she was far from "ugly." I wanted to speak to her after class regarding this. It never happened; a missed opportunity. One of my greatest regrets as a teacher.

Dear Dewey,

Locking up my classroom for the weekend, I see a large hand-made poster in the hallway just outside my door that some students placed there. It reads, "Dr. Shelnutt, You're the Bill of Rights to My Constitution." I feel loved ... I think.

Dear Dewey,

Most of the time, I make an effort to be outside of my classroom standing at the door during the passing period. This gives me a chance to greet students as they come in, say "hi" to former students, and give a warm smile to students I have never met.

Today I was standing by my door when a former student walked by. I see her most days as she makes her way down the hall to her next class. She stopped to talk to me. She mentioned how she had watched the movie, *The Godfather*, this past weekend. Grinning ear-to-ear, I exclaimed that I thought that was great. (*The Godfather* is my all-time favorite movie.) She said that since I had mentioned it so many times during the course of the school year that she thought she should probably watch it. Really? I mean, I know I don't shy away from telling the students such information when they ask, and I have a poster with a quote from the movie, ("Now you come and say 'Don Corleone, give me justice.' But you don't ask with respect. You don't offer friendship. You don't even think to call me 'Godfather.'" Somehow it sums up my relationship to my students, and theirs to me.) It's not like I make references to the movie on a regular basis. I asked her what she thought, and she said that she liked it. I was telling her about parts II and III when she jumped in and said she binge watched all three.

Sometimes as I stand by my door, I can't help wondering if my life has meaning; if I am making an impact in the lives of my students. I thank God for moments like the one I shared today with Kim over *The Godfather*. Yes, my life has meaning. And if my students don't remember a thing I teach them, hopefully they will remember to "leave the gun; take the cannoli."

Dear Dewey,

I received an email informing me, by name, that I was no longer being considered for a particular job. This would have been disappointing, but fine, except I never applied. You know times are hard when complete strangers seek you out to let you know they don't want you.

Dear Dewey,

I am not sure if people realize it or not, but there's a fairly big turn-over in education. There are numerous reasons for it, and I don't see it changing any time soon. I know in our district, we have a hard time hanging on to our staff. Again, a number of reasons for that.

　　　As I see so many new faces this year, I can't help but think of former colleagues. Most of my closest "homies" have moved on to other places. I wonder what they are doing, and how they are faring. As my mind reminisces, I recall a teacher with whom I shared a classroom my first year in public education. We were both young, but that's where the commonality ends. She was very much the classic "liberal," and I the conservative in the purest sense (too much, I am ashamed to admit). Dawn was known for coming in Monday morning and sharing with her students how she spent the weekend spiking trees to discourage logging. Other weekends she was out with Greenpeace saving the whales by ramming boats. Here I was doing yard work, enjoying my young sons, and playing board games with my wife's and my friends.

It was amidst this environment that an early sweet memory in education was fostered for me. I was leaving my classroom for the period so Dawn could use it. She had placed a box for students to put worksheets and paper they were no longer going to use. This was in the early days of recycling; before it was a cool thing to do. I noticed she had a sign on the makeshift recycle box she had created—it read, "White Paper Only." As I left the room, with no students present, I went into a pretend rant, saying that I could not believe she would only accept recycle paper from her white students. I kept a straight face, but then we both had a good laugh. Dawn and I would never be aligned politically, but God bless her, we knew how to keep it civil and appreciate one another.

Another memory I have of Dawn isn't as sweet. We were at a faculty meeting. I sat at a table with Dawn and three other teachers. Something was said that got her fuming. At that moment one of the male teachers looked across the table and said to Dawn, "I love how your breasts heave when you're angry." If they weren't heaving before, they sure were after that comment. Now, this was the late 80's, and people weren't as hyper politically correct as they are now, but even then it shocked me that my colleague had said this.

I wonder what happened to him. I wonder what Dawn is doing these days.

Dear Dewey,

"This is the way the world ends

Not with a bang but a whimper."

- Me (quoting T.S. Eliot to my seniors as I let them know how they did on their last   Economics chapter test)

Dear Dewey,

School was out for the day and I'd just finished grading the assignments my students had turned in. As I prepared to get on the road for my daily return commute, I decided to make a quick trip to the Men's Faculty Restroom. I went through the first of two doors into the bathroom to find a student standing there. He seemed more than a bit nervous, and stammered when I asked what he was doing there. Without a decent explanation, I told him he needed to leave, which he did hesitantly. I then proceeded through the second swinging door to the inner sanctum of the Men's Room. At that moment I discovered a male student hiking up his pants, and a female student in the stall doing the same. Of all the places on campus that you could pick to fool around, and there are plenty, the faculty restroom seems like it would be near the bottom of the list. Freshmen are so lacking in their

judgment.

Dear Dewey,

Today a student asked me when I decided to become a teacher. I've

been asked this many times before, so my standard, "When I was in

elementary school" came quickly. The student gave the typical

surprised response, and then went back to what she was doing. As I sit

here at the end of the day, looking over rows of empty desks, I give

greater pause and wonder, "How did I get here?"

    I can remember my kindergarten teacher in Florida, Mrs. Frost.

I can't say I recall anything she taught me, but I can tell you all about

the time she let me bring my dog, Barney, in for Show-and-Tell. Oh,

and naps on a vinyl mat. Good times. The following year I moved

across the street to the elementary school with the big kids and my

three older siblings. My mother also volunteered as the school nurse,

as she was an RN who was now a stay-at-home mom, giving her life to nurture her children. My next teacher was Mrs. St. John. I could recount all kinds of stories from that year, but I know I must have enjoyed her class because when my parents told us we would be moving to New York the next year, I cried. Not because I'd be leaving my friends, but because I'd be leaving Mrs. St. John. (Think "Miss Crabtree" from *The Little Rascals*.)

When I moved to New York, my educational experience was varied. Entering the second grade at Little Neck Elementary, I clearly was the new kid in town. I didn't sound like the other kids, having a Southern drawl. In class, whenever the answer to a math equation was "10," the teacher called on me, because I'd pronounce it as "tan." I'm sure that didn't happen every time, but that's how I remember it. I guess New Yorkers didn't like how this Southern boy talked, because I soon found myself pulled out of class to attend speech lessons. I no longer have my drawl, but I don't sound like a New Yorker, either. Small victories. The next two years saw a couple more teachers (all female), and then I transferred to a different elementary school since Little Neck only went through the fourth grade. Not only that, but after finishing fourth grade, the district closed the school. I'd like to think I had something to do with that.

At Thomas J. Lahey Elementary, I had my first male teacher, Mr. Gallagher. As for looks, he was the 70's version of Billy Connolly. He commanded the room with his voice and wit. If you weren't paying attention during a lesson, or messing around, he'd walk around the room to get to your desk and thump you with his class ring (a practice that would get him fired today, no doubt). He took lunch orders calling milk "moo juice." But you knew he cared. When the class bully broke his arm at recess, a concerned Mr. Gallagher picked him up in his arms and carried him to the nurse's office. I loved going to his class every day. When you get right down to it, I have always had a love of learning. I just have an innate desire to know and discover, and Mr. Gallagher fed that desire on a daily basis.

By the 5th and 6th grades, I knew I wanted to be a teacher. Maybe it was having male teachers in both those grades that showed me how it could be. I loved the school environment and wanted it to be a part of my life always. Growing up during my "formative years" in

New York helped to feed my love of learning, especially for history. Our class would go on field trips numerous times throughout the year. My favorites were the historically based ones. Going to villages that were recreations of colonial times. Visiting homes built in the Revolutionary period. Walking through old cemeteries. These weren't just things in books—they were real. I could touch these relics. Those people who have gone before me … they were real. They had real lives, real desires and passions, and real disappointments.

I could go on through the junior high and high school years. I enjoyed most of the teachers I had. Even the ones that didn't scratch me where I itched still taught me a thing or two. Now here I sit, so many years and so many students behind me, with an unknown number before me. At minimum, I want my students to become life-long learners. If they don't recall the causes of the French Revolution, they can still live long, fulfilled, productive lives. If they leave their twelve years of public education not hating history, and I had something to do with that, all the better. Because some come back to tell me, I know I have had an impact on a few students; at least a couple who have gone on to be history teachers themselves. I'd love to have that kind of impact on all my students, but I know that just isn't realistic. Perhaps generations from now the legacy of Mr. Gallagher will carry on. I wonder who his teacher was.

Dear Dewey,

Had to kill time while my car was being worked on, so I walked a few blocks to a Starbucks. I'm not really a fan, but there wasn't any other viable option. To get to the Starbucks I had to walk by the adjoining Wells Fargo Bank. Looking into the window I noticed a couple of carafes with complimentary coffee. I went in, fixed myself a cup and sat down in their comfortable and inviting waiting area. Free coffee, air conditioning, and a comfortable chair (not to mention a lot of extra attention from the manager and bank security) all for free! SCORE! (Take that Starbucks.)

Dear Dewey,

I love coffee. I don't see how anyone can be a public school teacher and not love this nectar of the gods. If I didn't have to plan and time my restroom breaks, I'd drink it all day long. It's not so much the caffeine kick I get from it, though that is a bonus; it's more of the earthy, warm taste and the delicious aroma. There have been periods when I would drink it black, and I still do if there are no accoutrements to go with it. I'm fine with straight cream and sugar, but I have been enjoying a special treat over the last few months.

First thing in the morning, I go into the teacher workroom where a couple coffee makers have been set up. Having paid a small annual fee to become part of the "coffee club" entitles the member, ME, to all the coffee I can drink. The usual sugar, sugar substitute, and powdered cream are also included with my "membership," but I have my own special additive. A friend who is a fellow coffee snob introduced me to certain small containers that have concentrated flavorings for coffee. These small bottles fit easily into my satchel and come in a variety of flavors: vanilla, hazelnut, Irish crème, and amaretto, just to name a few.

Today I was in the workroom getting my first morning coffee. As I pulled out one of my flavorings and added the two simple drops needed, I was greeted by the principal. She asked how my morning was going, and how my school year was progressing. You know, educational chit-chat. Then the hammer came down. She asked what it was that I was putting in my coffee. I told her some flavor extract for my coffee, and after showing her the bottle in my hand, asked her if she wanted to try some. She chuckled and declined. She then told me that one of my colleagues had seen me putting these drops in my coffee for some time, and thought I had a drinking problem. Apparently, these little bottles resemble the small bottles of alcohol you can purchase on the airplane. While on the one hand I appreciate the concern, and the way the principal handled it, I was disappointed that my coworker didn't come speak with me in private. Show some genuine care and compassion and call for an intervention with my friends and family after the school day; don't rat me out to my boss. I guess I know who's not getting that bottle of Baileys for Christmas.

Dear Dewey,

Today I attended an after school meeting regarding one of my students. She has been at our school for only a few weeks, but has already run into some difficulties. Like a number of our students, she lives at a group home near the campus. The meeting was with many stake holders, including teachers and county support personnel.

When it came my time to share out what I had observed and how the student was progressing in my class, I explained her behavior could only be described as disruptive to the learning environment, and that she simply did no classwork. As I was mid-way through my input, one of our student advocates, Tony, came in to join the meeting. He had not been there for the first part of what I had presented, but he felt fully capable of speaking regarding the situation in my classroom with this student. Sitting behind me, Tony interrupted me and said that it wasn't that the student was not doing the work, but that she crammed all of her work into her backpack and failed to turn it in. Tony added that he knew this because he went through the student's backpack with her and found a handful of work. Keep in mind that this advocate has never stepped foot in my classroom to observe the student we were discussing. He has no idea what this student does or does not do. More than anything, I felt that Tony was being highly unprofessional in contradicting my report in front of this large group without knowing all the pertinent facts. I assured Tony and the group that what I had shared was accurate. Perhaps in other classes the student throws her finished work into her backpack, but I have kept an eye on the student, and she doesn't even take out a pencil to write with, let alone work on a single assignment.

Feeling the tension that was now in the room, the county representative asked if there was any work that the student could turn in late and still receive credit. I thought for a minute, because I do want the student to be successful in my class, but I do not let other students turn in late classwork, so I said none at this point. I explained my class policy regarding late work (I don't accept any since all work is done in class, not at home), and how it was an issue of equity for all my students. The county representative seemed satisfied with my answer, but Tony, still sitting behind me, asked, "Is that in your syllabus?" I felt like I was being grilled by an attorney who was trying to find some little loophole to get a favorable outcome for his client. I assured Tony that it was. Silence.

It's great that those in education want to advocate for students. It shows a lot of heart. But are we allowing students to feel the consequences of their choices if we allow them, or as in this case, directly help them, to avoid such consequences? This is a problem in general in the current environment of education. When anyone, student or otherwise, is told over and again that they have succeeded, even though they haven't achieved what was set before them—when "everyone gets a trophy"— then we are inadvertently breeding a society that feels entitled and simply does not know how to deal with failure, rejection, difficulties, or pain.

May

Education is the key to unlock the golden door of freedom.

– George Washington Carver

Dear Dewey,

It never ceases to amaze me the kind of information and knowledge students expect teachers to have. Grant it, many teachers will act like they are the gatekeepers to the mind of God, but for the most part, we're just ordinary folk. One secret, of course, is when a student asks you a subject-based question that you really should know but don't, one simply replies, "Now, now … let's not get ahead of ourselves. We'll be getting to that tomorrow." You now have 24 hours in which to get the answer.

Today we were discussing the flight of the first Space Shuttle. I had the opportunity to share with the students how I had tickets to be in the viewing stand that day (though we wisely chose to watch it from the beach just south of The Cape). One curious young lady raised her hand and asked, "How long does it take to build one of those." I immediately responded by saying, "Not long at all. I built one just last weekend in my backyard." She didn't even bat an eye or question the veracity of my answer. Man, I love my job!

Dear Dewey,

Dear School Counselor,

Please do not direct students to come to me asking if they can turn in months-old assignments when I have already told them from August, and several times since then, that they cannot. (And you have known my policy for over a decade.) I don't appreciate being made the bad guy.

Dear Dewey,

Came across an old report card from 2nd Grade in New York. (I'm pretty sure that teacher never liked me much. It might have been that

Southern Boy vs. Yankee thing.) I noticed the comments. "Max's sociability seems to interfere with his work. He could do better with a bit more effort." This explains A LOT. If only I had heeded her counsel. Besides, it was THE 2ND GRADE ... it's not like I was working on my M.A. or PhD. My grades weren't that bad. (Obviously, I was a beast at kickball in PE.)

Dear Dewey,

Over the last couple of years, I have made it a practice to go into the classrooms of a couple of my "school homies" and randomly bust out in a verse or two of a song; then I leave without a word. At first, this frightened a few of the students, who wondered who this strange man was. After a while, they'd see me coming down the hall toward their room and anticipate what was going to happen next. To their credit, my buddies were always very gracious and indulged me for the moment. I would do similar singing with my own students, but my choice of songs was usually tied to something going on in the class.

For instance, when we discuss the reunification of Germany in the 90's, I'll sing a few bars of "Reunited" by Peaches and Herb.

With this as a backdrop, a few months ago I had a knock on my door during my last class of the day. It was three of my students who handed me a book and said, "Here's your script. Your parts are marked with the Post-Its." Now, I had talked with the drama teacher a couple times about helping out with the annual musical productions, but I never dreamed I'd actually be given a part—and in this case, two (small) roles.

When I walked into the rehearsal room after school that day, the students warmly welcomed me with a simple, spontaneous, "Shelnutt!" That was the beginning of a journey unlike any I have been on before, and one which could likely fill an entire book. With the final curtain just a few days ago, my mind has become introspective on what I experienced.

The two main instructors of this event, our Theater teacher and the band director, were professional in the first degree. Never have I seen such hard work, diligence, and perseverance. When it was

"Spring Musical" season, neither got home until at least 8 p.m. each night, with most nights being much longer than that. They do not get paid extra for this, and though it is in some respect a part of their jobs, they clearly go above and beyond what most would expect.

These two heroes of the school and stage (and community) were only eclipsed by the students themselves. Now, my roles were small and relatively insignificant. However, the lead players had pages and pages of dialog to memorize, not to mention songs and choreography to nail down. For the secondary players, most had 3 or 4 roles to play. When someone was sick and could not be there for rehearsal (which was rare), someone else would step up and deliver the lines and sing the song spot on. I had no idea that these very same students who fill seats in my classroom and struggle through the hallways of adolescence, had such depth of talent and commitment. Though most alumni will remember the name of the star quarterback of the football team, few will remember "Girl #3" in the school play, although both put forth incredible effort and work.

Having acknowledged all of the above, what still resonates with me personally is how these same students extended such grace and patience with *me*. Now, when I sing in my own classes, or go visit a colleague, I will only sing that with which I feel comfortable, which is limited being I have a very narrow range. The small and brief singing part that I had was very challenging for me, and my old ears had a hard time hearing the notes correctly. The music director had to go over my part with me time and again. At one point he even had the students sing a section so I could hear it better. In all of this, not once did the students roll their eyes or scoff. In the rehearsal room and behind stage, I have never felt so supported. I might have been schooled by my students, but in the best way imaginable.

Dear Dewey,

Picked up some take-out Chinese food for dinner tonight. Instructions on wrapper of chopsticks: "(Step 1) Tuck under thumb and hold firmly. (Step 2) Add second chopstick, hold it as you hold a pencil.

(Step 3) Hold first chopstick in original position, move the second one up and down, now you can pick up anything." Well, it's a lie. I did as they said, and attempted to pick up the front end of my car. All I got for my effort was disappointment, a few splinters, and several concerned looks from the neighbors.

Dear Dewey,

After handing in her last AP unit test to me today, one of my students quietly took out her deodorant stick and, reaching under her shirt, judiciously applied it. That, my friends, is when you know you've given a good exam.

Dear Dewey,

In the early days of a new school year, my students and I are in need of time to get to know each other. Eventually students will want to share personal information, such as what they are going to do over the weekend, or perhaps a movie they recently saw. Throughout the year I try to interject tidbits now and then, to help them see me as another human being. It's funny when they see you at the store or a restaurant; somehow they think we never leave the school campus (and sometimes it feels that way to me, too). We exchange these insights into our lives not so that we can become buddies; students don't need teachers who are their buddies. I made that mistake in my first year of teaching, as do most newbie teachers. Students do, however, need to know that you are a person who has highs and lows just like they do. They need to know you are genuine and approachable.

It was in this spirit that as we were having a lighter moment in class that I blurted out, "And you know, I am an ordained minister. So, if you ever need someone to do your wedding, I can hook you up." There was the typical look of stun and confusion. Most of the students know that I have my doctorate, but they assume it is a medical doctor (some think that is the only kind of doctor), and a few might think it is in history or education. Having peaked their interest for a moment, I tell them that I did a wedding for two former students years ago. "Yep.

And they are still together. I'd like to think I have something to do with that. And they have a couple kids, I believe, but I didn't have anything to do with that." A few of the sharper students will pick up on the last part.

Every year I'll get a student who will come into class, just aching to ask the question, "Dr. Shelnutt, I heard you used to be a model. Is that true?" I never know the source of their information, but somehow it gets passed on year after year. I usually lead them on a bit, asking, "Why would you ask such a thing?" Still not revealing their source, the student will give a generic, "Oh, I just heard that. Is it true?" The short answer is, yes—kind of. When I was first married, I did some Saturday classes in San Francisco in hopes of securing an agent to do some commercials or even television. I had always wanted to get into the entertainment business, and I figured I'd give it a shot. When I signed up for the classes, they thought I should do some of the modeling modules, too. It was fun for me, and a money making venture for the company that preyed on the dreams of young people. Out of this I got a photo season with a professional photographer to help start my portfolio, a stack of black and white head-shots, and one paid gig—I was a fit-model for a men's clothing line. A fit-model is basically a living mannequin on which a designer develops his product. Not as exciting as being an underwear model for a leading magazine, but it was a paying gig.

The students often find that hard to believe, especially when they see before them a past-midlife specimen. I still have a few of those black and white head shots, and a couple of the pictures from that photo shoot. When I present these as evidence, I usually hear a few gasps of disbelief; with the usual comment from one of the boys, "That's not you." When I point out a couple identifying marks, there is a moment of silence. Then, inevitably, one of the girls will say, "Dang, Shelnutt, you used to look good." I'm never sure if I should be thrilled or hurt by that response. I'll assume the best and take the former for now—we're still getting to know each other.

Dear Dewey,

While grading papers, I came across one that in the place for "Name" the words "Your gay!" was written (clearly, a buddy of the student had scratched it on there). Using my red pen, I put a line through the words for their inappropriateness, and then wrote, "You mean 'You're' not 'Your'." Gotta grab those teachable moments when you can.

Dear Dewey,

For the past two years I have had the privilege of teaching seniors (Economics and American Government). This age group is fun, as they are starting to tune in to issues beyond what they are going to do this weekend, and they understand most of my jokes. The down-side is many check-out far too soon and come to the point that they might not pass the class—which means they don't graduate. This results in very difficult phone calls to parents (who mostly blame me).

Such was the case of one of my current seniors, Billy. I let Billy and his father know that Billy was in grave danger of failing and not graduating. He would need to excel in the remainder of assignments, and score a 90% or better on both the last unit exam, as well as the final. Now, my tests are embarrassingly easy, being taken directly from the classwork and usually involve a series of matching and multiple choice questions (the students, in essence, have the test in advance). Well, Billy hasn't passed a single unit exam this semester, so passing this last one was huge for him. He showed up to my room before school for some last minute studying. He showed me the notes he had made, including a handwritten "practice test." I assured him that these were fine tools and practices. He was buzzing.

Two hours later came test time. Billy took his test, and turned it in with a sense of confidence I had not seen from him before. All tests were turned in, and I scanned them during the class time. I called the name of every student asking the students if they wanted me to call out their score (or they can come up and see it in private). Billy gave me permission to call out his grade … "100%." There was a collective gasp from his classmates.

As I recorded the grades into my online grade book, I could hear Billy showing and explaining to the other students what he had done to prepare, just as he had done two hours earlier with me. You would have thought he had won the Super Bowl or a Nobel Peace Prize in Government. I guess, in some ways, he had.

Dear Dewey,

Arriving home today I stopped by the community mailbox to get my mail. My box was stuffed, mainly due to one of those soft-sided, plastic packages. I thought, "I don't recall ordering anything," but assumed a friend had sent me a surprise gift. Hey, it happens. I got home and pried a hole into the defiant plastic, reached my hand in only to pull out a coral-colored 38DD laced bra. I immediately realized this wasn't mine; I'm only a C-cup. So, to my neighbor who will find this previously opened package on your stoop this evening, if there is a God in heaven, I pray we will never meet in person. My face will turn a darker shade than your bra.

Dear Dewey,

There is an oft repeated "fact" that says that due to the relatively small size of their wings in ratio to their bodies, bumble bees should not be able to fly. It is said that every time one flies, they are shattering the world of physics. This is, of course, false, but just hearing it again today made me think of so many of my students.

Sometimes students come to me with what appears to be intellectual and academic tiny wings. It might be how they perform on the first unit exam, the lack of insight from the assignments they turn in, their unusually quiet demeanor in class (or just the opposite —their disruptively loud chatter), handwriting that looks like some ancient, undeciphered language, or even something as simple as their body language and posture. I had a professor tell me when I was going through my teacher education program that I should look over the academic records of all my students as soon as I get my roster in August so I can see who the winners and losers were.

It is hard not to pre-judge. Does the class clown really have anything to offer? If Gary had any wits about him, would he be more responsible and have his homework done and turned in on time? Sadly, many of these "types" seem to bear out and promote the pre-labeling. The question I have to ask myself, "Am I just creating a self-fulfilling prophecy? Do these students stay in their rut, if they were in one to begin with, simply because no one, including me, is projecting a vibe that they can and will succeed?"

I currently have a sophomore who practically failed every class as a freshman. Right now, he has A's and B's. He's proud of that fact, as well he should be. He mentioned how he was determined to do better this year. I had no idea of his previous struggles. I'm glad I hadn't looked at his transcript. Perhaps I would have treated him differently.

Teachers, parents, and students need to look beyond the small wings. They can fly—it just might not be the same physics of, say, an airplane. But oh, how they can fly.

Dear Dewey,

Sally was one of those students most teachers are just not sure what to think of when they first meet her. I met her as a senior in my Economics class. She was a special needs student who desired to graduate early (at the end of the first semester). Sally was very open and vocal in class, admitting that she had spent a significant part of her childhood homeless on the streets. She was also personally familiar with the world of drugs, including during her brief time at our school. Even in the midst of all this, she usually had the broadest smile on her face, and was always ready to be a part of the class discussions. During her semester with me she turned 18, which meant she could sign herself in and out of school. She wore the age badge proudly, and even mentioned it when it had little-to-no significance to the topic at hand (especially in her caseworker meetings).

Educators try to instill the most they can into their students while they have them. Some, to be sure, are more difficult to reach, but you try. Sally and I got along just fine, even though her outbursts and endless monologues tried my patience at times. All things considered, she was a genuine tender heart. When I looked at Sally two thoughts filled my mind: despite her experience, there was a childlike innocence about her, and she is a student I can see living most of her adult life under a bridge somewhere.

Today I received an email from the principal. Sally's body was found behind a dumpster at a local "big box" store. There was apparent head trauma. I'm shocked, and I'm not. Angry. Heaviest of hearts. Nothing prepares you for this kind of news. I search for answers; none are forthcoming.

Dear Dewey,

I was walking past the various wings and rooms today dealing with my first-of-the morning tasks. Trekking by the Main Office rooms, I stopped to say good morning. Jim replied in kind, and we chatted a bit about the weekend. As I was getting ready to leave, he fumbled with a stack of papers and said, "Oh, Max, I wanted to let you know we are moving you to another classroom next year." Jim told me the building it would be in, but could not confirm the specific room just yet. I acknowledged the news and went on my way. For most this would be business as usual, but for me it hit hard.

For a couple years now there has been a desire by others to have me move classrooms, even giving me the option to do so, but I have always turned down the offer. When talk of shifting rooms to align the departments first started, one individual assured me I would not have to move, and even punctuated the promise by saying, "Do you want me to put it in writing, Max?" Whenever anyone asks you, "Do you want me to put it in writing?" always respond with, "That would be great. Thanks."

Never once have I been asked why I held on to my room so tenaciously. The decision makers assume it is because I do not want the hassle of moving my stuff, or because I am unwilling to change. While these things might be true, these are not the main reasons. See, Dewey, I have been in that room from the first day I started at this school. It has been over ten years—longer than I have been in any house in my life. A month after I started at the school, my wife became ill, resulting in a life-long mental disability. Home life would now be unstable and tumultuous. The one thing I could count on in my life was what took place in the world that was Room 2022. Over the years it became iconic and identified with me. Students, many of whom were not my own, ate their lunch there every day—just because. Students would come back to visit years later, surprising me in the midst of class instruction. The first thing they would do as they walked through the door would be to look around like a child first visiting Disneyland, taking in all the sights, and saying, "I really miss this room."

Having me move actually makes practical, institutional sense. I do not argue with the reasoning behind these changes, and hold no bitterness over the purpose of the decision. I was told, however, of the impending change in locations by chance. I just happened to be walking down the right hallway at the right time. I do not mind so much the work of moving my stuff and taking down the dozens of posters that hearken the bland walls, and I do not run from change, but when you move me you strip a bit of my identity from me. I will move, fix up the next room best I can, but please don't just see me like a piece on a chess board. Find out why my face has a look of despair. Take the time to look me straight in my eyes and see me as a person who puts everything he has into his chosen profession. In room 2022.

June

Children need to get a high-quality education, avoid violence and the criminal-justice system, and gain jobs. But they deserve more. We want them to learn not only reading and math but fairness, caring, self-respect, family commitment, and civic duty.

– Colin Powell

Dear Dewey,

Today in preparation for the upcoming finals, my class and I were discussing the revolutions of the early 19th Century. Not one of my favorite eras, but it is part of our curriculum. At one point, I explained to the students, through a Power Point lecture, how France crossed the Pyrenees into Spain and the Austrian Empire crossed over the Alps into modern day Italy to put down rebellions that were seeking independence and national identity. In my delivery I pointed out that this was done on foot and on horseback; there were no trains, planes, or trucks to make the trip easier.

Part of the presentation, of course, includes pictures. Students are very visual; I suppose most of us are. When I put up an aerial photograph of the Alps and emphasized that the Austrians had to cross them to put down the rebellion, a student spoke out and asked, "Then how could they take that picture (if there were no planes)?" The class immediately busted up and cast less-than-supportive words her way. It was hard not to laugh; not from the humiliation and taunting, but from her innocent, albeit misguided, insight.

From an educator's perspective, her contribution showed she was listening. She made the connection that the photographer did not have those modern means of transportation, so how could he take the picture. She lacked the connection to the fact that the picture was a current picture, but it demonstrated she was engaged. For that, she should be praised.

This episode reminds me of something I stumbled across once. I read that if a person mispronounces a word or name, don't criticize; it only means she learned the word by reading (as opposed to being told how the word sounds). I thought this was an interesting insight and a good rule by which to live. We are all learning, though we may be at different points. To put someone down who is behind you in his learning is the height of arrogance. It implies you are superior; as if you were not a learner yourself (and continue to be one).

It was a great reminder for me. I want my classroom to be a place where it is safe to be a learner. God help me, and give me the wisdom to know how to create such a space for all my students.

Dear Dewey,

The regular coffee person at work forgot to make coffee today. How do they expect me to function under these conditions? I should just call it a day and go home at this point.

Dear Dewey,

Educators expect that in every class there will be a mix of personalities. Though I am a teacher who tries to be as objective as I possibly can be, and provide each student with the same opportunity for success and the same unbiased nurturing as any other student in the room, there always seems to be that one student who makes it his or her purpose in life to irritate the teacher beyond reason. This type of student is like a mite that burrows under one's skin and drives the victim to the brink of insanity no matter what is done to change the situation. Gerald was one such mite.

Gerald was a senior who had only months before he left the comforts and protection of public education. I say "comforts and protection" because there are some students' behaviors that if done outside these walls, would be met with the harshest and most violent response from others. In other words, they'd get the crap beat out of them. But here, we counsel them, try to get them to make "better choices," and can do little more than talk to them about their anti-social behavior. They know it, and take full advantage of it.

This young man did the typical annoying things found in just about any public school classroom in the United States. He talked loudly whenever he felt the urgency to do so, used language that was far from appropriate, and treated me with utter contempt. He, along with his other partners in crime, even came up with what they called

"The Shelnutt Dance." No, this was not some sweet homage to their instructor, but a way to daily display in a camouflaged manner their disrespect. There were other things Gerald did, seemingly effortlessly, to be the bane of my existence. I recall standing outside my classroom at the door at the start of class, as I do most days, and just the sound of his voice as he entered our wing started my stomach acid boiling.

I believe the low point (or would that be the high point for Gerald) came when my daughter had asked if she could come to school with me. She must have been 9 or 10 at the time. I informed my classes the day before her visit, and encouraged their best behavior. For Gerald's class, I added the note that they should refrain from using profanity while my daughter was there. As I looked toward Gerald's direction, he pantomimed how he would welcome my daughter—by "making moves" on her, putting his arm around her, and sexually assaulting her. Truth be known, the public servant part of me struggled ferociously with the father part of me. Losing my job and spending some time in prison almost seemed worth it at the moment. Yet somehow I was supposed to go ahead with the day's Economics lesson after such a display.

Now why all this talk about Gerald today? It's been years since he harkened these halls. Though he is long gone, every year brings a new batch of mites. Don't get me wrong, most students are fantastic and are maturing into fine young adults. It is a blessing and privilege to be able to pour into their lives. Very few reach the level of mitehood, and even less to the lowly obnoxiousness that Gerald had obtained. With the few mites that do surface, I always wonder, "What will happen to them when they leave here?" If the light never goes on, if they remain in this stage of arrested development, how will they survive? What will their lives look like? Will they find a mate, and with what will their relationship be filled? Will they live long enough to regret some of their earlier behavior, as I have had a couple return to apologize, or will they be cut down by someone who refused to take their antics any longer? As I deal with a few of my current challenging students, my mind always goes to Gerald. Whatever became of him? I mean, you can't make a living doing "The Shelnutt Dance." I tried once to have a genuine discussion with him regarding his future. I pulled him aside and asked him if he had ideas about what the future held for him. To my surprise, his answer was both sober and articulate. Gerald said he wanted to be a policeman. The only thing that went through my mind at that moment was, "Good Lord, don't anyone give this guy a gun." Still, I wonder …

Dear Dewey,

So, during the last few days of school, my students end up playing a select number of class-wide games. In one class, AP World History, I had the class in 4 teams of five, playing "Trivial Pursuit, Jr.". The question to one team was, "What happens to water at 32 degrees Fahrenheit?" Everyone in the room saw this as a "give-me" question. A slam-dunk. No one could understand why there wasn't an immediate response, but rather frantic discussion among the team. Certainly, at least one person in five knew the answer. This was, after all, an AP class. With only seconds left on the clock (they get 30 seconds to give an answer), the spokesperson gave the team answer: "Evaporates?" All I can say is don't blame me; I teach history, not science.

Dear Dewey,

A couple days ago I recounted my encounters with a former student named Gerald. Though he was anything but a young person who commanded respect, he had desires to enter into law enforcement, a career for which I have the highest respect. Today I had a similar experience with a current student.

Juan is not the loud disrupter that Gerald was. No, he is more of one of those who goes along with the group of malcontents, quietly in the background. Sure, he'll talk at times when he isn't supposed to, but he's more of a sidekick than the lead man. When his cohorts are absent, Juan is almost pleasant to have in the room. At the very least, he is not part of disrupting the educational community.

Like Gerald so many years ago, I pulled Juan aside to have a heart-to-heart with him. This wasn't to correct some bad behavior in class, or to shame him for doing so poorly on his last exam. No, I genuinely wanted to know what his plans were for the near future, if he had any. I first asked Juan if he was planning on graduating, if that was a desire of his, since his current grades did not reflect that (not just in my class, but in others as well). As a senior, he doesn't have as many "safety nets" and re-dos as underclassmen might be afforded. He assured me that he hoped to graduate, though his progress and even the less-than-enthusiastic way he replied seem to betray that dream. Accepting his desire to graduate as being legitimate, I asked what post-high school life held for him. What does Juan want to do when he is no longer by law required to participate in public, compulsory education? He softly, yet unapologetically said, "I plan to be a painter." By painter Juan didn't mean an artist like Rembrandt or Picasso. No, he meant a house painter. He went on to explain that his uncle did that for a living, and that Juan was going to be an apprentice of sorts under his uncle.

What could I say—he had a plan, a trajectory. I try to let my students know that it's okay for them not to go to college. It doesn't make them of any less value as a person. Teachers try to prepare all students so that college will be an option for them (simply called "college-readiness" in educational circles), but that isn't the pathway for all. This country also needs tradesmen, and there is even a current shortage in my state of those who are pursuing a career in any number of trades. It also struck me that technically Juan doesn't need a high school diploma to pursue his chosen career. That said, a K-12 diploma isn't just about how that piece of paper will further your career goals— it's about nurturing a young adult to be whole, multi-dimensional, and one who will contribute to our society. Sometimes we forget that. I thank God for moments like I had with Juan. They help keep me centered, and pushing on for the sake of the Juans, and yes even the Geralds, of tomorrow.

Dear Dewey,

It was a rough day and I decided to have a little fun at a local coffee shop that sponsored a karaoke night. Man, was it rough. Two teenage girls giving it their all on Queen's "Bohemian Rhapsody." All I could do was silently pray, "Help them, Jesus." Well, sometimes God says, "No."

Dear Dewey,

Today a colleague said I was being "snarky." This is not a word I am used to hearing or using, and I wasn't sure how to respond, so I just said, "Oh yeah?!"

Dear Dewey,

The campus where I currently teach is a typical California school campus in that it is open. That is, there are numerous buildings or wings that require you walk outdoors to get from one place to the next. As such, there are many times throughout the day that requires students and teachers to open a glass door to enter the building. I wouldn't even try to estimate how many times a day I pass through these doors.

Opening so many doors leads to multiple opportunities to hold the door wide for others. Since the students far outnumber the number of staff members, simple math will tell you that when I am holding a door for someone, it is more than likely a student. I welcome these opportunities, as it is a small way of displaying mutual respect. Unfortunately, that mutual respect does not always travel down both sides of the road. I would guess that about seven out of every ten students I hold the door for will pass through without even acknowledging my presence. No eye contact. Not even a low mumbled, "Thanks." Perhaps they think the doors are automatic like those at a department store. Seriously, the attitude with which many of these students saunter through would only be surpassed by the haughtiest of divas at an awards show. I almost want to look around to see if I can get a view of their body guards and entourage. Sometimes I kid myself in thinking I will use this as a teachable moment and simply offer a "You're welcome" as they scurry past me. I wish I were that high-minded. It's just my passive-aggressive way of airing my displeasure.

Now, before you think I'm just a tired old bitter teacher who needs to retire, and while that may be true, I have seen and acknowledge that there seems to be almost as many students who will see me coming to the door, and will stay to hold the door for me, or even hold it to allow me to pass through first. We need to affirm these young men and women, and give hope that these attitudes and behaviors will be what shapes the society of tomorrow.

Dear Dewey,

I am so thankful for the many promises of God. For instance, today I am especially thankful for the promise found in Proverbs 26:11, "As a dog returns to its vomit ..." Our beagle Zack was good enough to clean up after himself just as I was heading out to work. Man's best friend on a whole new level.

Dear Dewey,

In class today we played a trivia game. I ask a series of 6 questions, the answers to which all have some connection or theme in common that the students have to figure out. In one series, the first answer/clue was "head." The second answer/clue was "wood." All of a sudden my classroom was filled not with maturing young adults, but with pre-pubescent junior highers. Only 8 more school days. I can do this.

Dear Dewey,

I'm pretty sure that if Moses had been born in Gilmer, Texas, instead of in Egypt, pickled okra would have been manna (and if not pickled okra, then deep fried BBQ pork rinds … or maybe grits … or biscuits and sausage gravy). And when he struck the rock in the desert, it would have been sweet tea God provided, not water. Oh, how I do miss the Promised Land.

Dear Dewey,

Another year of teaching is almost in the books. It has been a difficult year both professionally and personally, especially the last few months. It will be forever etched in my memory as "The Year of Loss." I thank the good Lord for co-workers and students who brighten my day with moments here and there without even knowing it. The good thing about teaching is, August brings a new year with new possibilities; a blank page, so to speak (or in my case, a new overhead transparency).

Dear Dewey,

Last August, on the first day of class, I welcomed the students to the class, directed them to their assigned seats, and read through the class syllabus with them. The basic idea of the syllabus was to be a point of reference to let them know what to expect from the class, what to expect from me, what I expected from them, and how they could succeed in the class—whatever "succeed" meant to them.

When I asked for questions, one young lady, who had not smiled once since she walked in, stated she had heard that "everyone fails this class." She wasn't trying to be funny; she was very sincere. I assured her that in fact, most of my students would pass the class, though some students would likely fail. I reemphasized that the syllabus and all that I'd said was a road map to success, and I would help her, or any of the other students, to do as well as they desired, if they wanted my help. I asked her where she heard such a thing. She told me that a friend of hers told her that everyone fails my class. I didn't ask who that was, assuming it was a former student who did indeed fail, but gently told her not to stress; she would see that not everyone fails.

She passed the class. I reminded her today of her words the first day. I guess she can go back to her source and let him know that not everyone fails.

Dear Dewey,

The bittersweet feeling of another school year coming to a close, and saying goodbye to graduating seniors who I will likely never see again. Godspeed.

Dear Dewey

July

The function of education is to teach one to think intensively and to think critically. Intelligence plus character—that is the goal of true education.

– Martin Luther King, Jr

Dear Dewey,

Picking up after the dog prior to raking the leaves reminded me a bit of my childhood Easter egg hunts. And no, unlike those fun-filled days of ages past, no candy surprises were consumed.

Dear Dewey,

Summer school tends to assemble a genuine cornucopia of students. These will range from those who are dealing with too much teen angst to cope with their school work, to those who are so angry at the world that they refuse to cooperate in any manner, cutting off their noses to spite their faces. That said, though most students in summer school are more ready to make it work than when in the usual school year, I will have a few that will not endure to the end. Such is the mix I've had this summer.

A couple days ago we had made it through the day's lessons without too much resistance. We were down to the last two minutes of our two hour block when Joey just couldn't contain his rebellious spirit any longer. When he started "acting out," which is the educational politically correct way of saying he was being an anti-social pain in the ass, I tried to "redirect" him, which is educationese for "sit down and try to act like a human for just two more minutes." Joey continued with his behavior, adding to it a few select words directed toward me. Keeping my professional cool and knowing the bell was about to ring, I told him we'd deal with this after class. Joey loudly proclaimed, "Let's step outside and deal with it right now." Every set of student eyes in that room shifted from Joey, to me, to Joey. While I could feel my natural adrenaline response welling up inside of me, I refrained and simply took out a referral form. I said, "Well, if that's how you want to play this out. Poor choice, Joey."

The bell rang as I began to write up the referral. The students filed out of the room, softly speaking of the events that just transpired. I've only had a student physically threaten me a couple times. I'm no action hero star, but at 6'1" I'm no slouch, so for the most part students only try to attack me verbally. I wrote down the pertinent information and concluded by saying, "I felt physically threatened by the student." While this was true, I'm not sure why I included it; I've never written anything like that before. A day later, the summer school principal said that she had set up a conference with the student and his mother. This ought to be good.

Today was the conference. The principal explained the basic information, and then allowed me to fill in any details that were needed. The mother, who was visibly not happy to be there, began to verbally confront both me and the principal. From her perspective, we had clearly conspired against her angel. When it was Joey's time to give his recollection of the story, it was a profanity-laced tirade that had little to do with the actual event. I've never been in a conference when the student let loose like this kid did. He clearly had watched too many Quentin Tarantino films starring Samuel L. Jackson. The mother just sat there, affirming her son's behavior with her silence.

The principal thanked the mother for coming in and excused both her and Joey. She then looked at me, both of us wanting to say, "What just happened?" To a degree, I felt vindicated; it wasn't just me being overly sensitive after a long day, which is something teachers are always fearful of happening. Then the principal put my options before me, adding some information that I did not know. Apparently Joey is a "frequent flyer" during the regular school year, having gotten into trouble often, and has already built up quite the long rap sheet. "Well, Dr. Shelnutt, since he threatened a district employee, he can be put up for expulsion (i.e. kicked out of not only summer school, but regular school). Or, if you prefer, he can be dropped from summer school." Despite what many students think, teachers are by-and-large merciful at heart. I said I just wanted him out of my class. It was done.

I've never really been concerned about any kind of retribution from a student, but until summer school ends, I'll wonder if he will be waiting for me in the parking lot, or if I will walk out to my car only to find my tires slashed. I suppose these are just the occupational hazards of teaching.

Dear Dewey,

I'm not sure which is the more disingenuous look of shock and surprise—the beauty contestant when she is told she has won the Miss America Pageant, or the customer who has just unloaded her shopping cart full of items onto the checkout stand only to be told she is in the "Express Lane – 20 Items or Less" aisle.

Dear Dewey,

Spent a part of the day at a memorial service. The room was filled with folks from many different ethnic groups, religious beliefs (and non-beliefs), different socio-economic positions, sexual preferences, males and females, and political views across the spectrum. Not a single pew was overturned, no fire bombs launched, no hate speech iterated, and no punches were thrown. There were, however, hugs and smiles exchanged, even among strangers, a meal shared, memories exchanged, and conversations genuinely seeking to know the person sitting across the table. King Solomon said, "It is better to go to a house of mourning than to go to a house of feasting, because that is the end of every man, and the living takes it to heart" (Eccl 7:2). Sounds like Solomon was indeed a wise man and ruler, and our nation as a whole could use a dose of what I experienced today.

Dear Dewey,

I took the day off from work. I think that was the first time I have done so during a summer school session. Had a root canal; the second root canal on that particular tooth (I didn't know that was even possible). It's all fun and games until you start smelling and seeing smoke.

Dear Dewey,

Today I was covering the Second Industrial Revolution with my summer school students. In mentioning the three social classes that developed during this time in Europe, I noted the "Upper Class, Middle Class, and the workers and peasants." As the students dutifully wrote down the notes from the PowerPoint, I said with the best dead-pan I could muster, "And we get the word 'peasants' from the fact that they were so poor, they had to eat peas and ants." The expressions of genuine excitement of discovery, and perhaps an interest in history for the first time for some, were worth the momentary lie.

Dear Dewey,

Weekend Check List:

Pick up dog poop in the yard

Fix the fence

Tear up old sod, haul away, replace with landscape rock

Clean out gutters

Organize garage

Do laundry

Repair non-working fan/overhead lighting

Give dog a bath

Paint (touch up) in guest bedroom

Feeling accomplished!

Okay, so I didn't get around to doing any of these, but I DID make a list. Yep, feeling accomplished!

Dear Dewey,

I've been telling students how many days are left of summer school (both as celebration and as motivation). After today, we have four days left. As I mentioned this at the close of class this morning, two students corrected me by saying the last day is July 22 (giving us nine days left). I then had to reassure them that, as I have been saying for over a week, the last day is July 15. Their jaws dropped. See, this course is all done on computers and is self-paced (requiring discipline). Apparently, THEIR pace can be counted off by a four year old learning how to count. Something likened to the little girl in the classic 1964 "Daisy" presidential ad. (Look it up, Dewey.)

Dear Dewey,

In a world of Hi-Def cell phones, mine makes calls in black and white.

Dear Dewey,

The summer session is drawing to close. Only a couple days left. We all, teachers and students alike, are counting the hours to the conclusion. Though there might be a few percentage points here and there that could slightly move a student's grade, for the most part the grades are set. That is unless there is pressure that comes from further upstream.

I spoke with my summer school colleague next door as I was leaving for the day. He has become a friend over the last several weeks, and seems to be an educator who genuinely cares about the young lives put into his charge. On top of a caring, compassionate heart is a young man who knows his subject matter and how to instruct young minds; a rare individual, indeed. He's been with the district only two years, so I hope he stays with us for a while. We lose so many of the good ones.

As I walked by his classroom and gave my customary, "We made it through another one. Have a great afternoon," I could see Pete wasn't his normal jovial self. I stepped fully into his room and asked if he had a rough day. He said the students were more antsy than usual, but they were fine. I pressed further, saying his countenance was different. He admitted he was having a tough time processing a visit he just had from the summer school principal. I put my things down and sat in a student desk next to his. I was not prepared to hear what he told me.

It seems there is a student in Pete's class that is not doing well. In fact, this student is failing miserably with a 30%. With only two days left to the summer session, it is simply mathematically impossible for this student to pass. Pete let me know that the student has been a thorn in his flesh from the first day. The student does very little work, which in summer school tends to be much less rigorous than the regular school year, and is a constant source of disruption to the class. I've had such students, but they usually stop coming by the end of the second week. Still this did not account for Pete's long face. The student had proven he was not committed to the learning opportunity he was given, and would suffer the consequence of his choices. Apparently, I spoke my end-of-the-year good-bye blessing too soon.

Minutes before I had passed the classroom, the summer school principal came and had a chat with Pete. Mr. Baringer asked about the aforementioned student's progress. Pete gave him the same report he had just given to me. Baringer matter-of-factly told my friend that the student needed to pass. Pete again reiterated that the student had not done the work, nor had he met the requirements for passage for the class. In no uncertain terms, the summer school principal let this young teacher know that this student needed to pass, and was going to pass. What was Pete to do? As stated above, he is only two years into the district, and about seven weeks away from being granted tenure. If Pete stood his ground, he might not have a job come August. After some initial hemming and hawing, Pete told the principal that he might reconsider some of the assignments the student had turned in and possibly pass him with a D-. According to Baringer, that simply would not do; the student needed to pass with a C. Convinced that the conversation had concluded, the principal left. Minutes later, I walked by.

As I sit here, I don't blame Pete for giving in to Baringer's demands. I probably would have done the same. For those who argue that tenure is a protection for bad teachers, they need to consider who else it might protect; teachers like Pete who want to do the right thing without fear of reprisal from bullying administrators. On one level, I don't even blame Baringer (but only on one level). I don't know what the motivation was that drove him to insist that the student pass, and pass with a C, but it likely came from further upstream. If we pull back from the trees and look at the forest for just a moment, we'll see that this is not a summer school issue, it is a societal issue. We have gotten to the point where we do not let an individual, in this case a summer school student, face the consequences of his actions. Somehow we have come to believe that giving someone a taste of success, devoid of any real accomplishment, will drive that individual to desire to succeed next time. Couple that with the desire to shield our children from ever failing at anything, and we are creating a generation, and eventually a society, that will not know how to deal with disappointment and consequences. We need to consider our endgame. From here, it's not looking so good.

Dear Dewey,

This diary and year is coming to an end. As I look over these pages, and think back to the faces and events that have contributed to making this year what it was, I want to end on a note of introspection. These are words that I would hope my students would embrace, but ones that I cling to for my own well-being.

What I was

       I no longer am.

What I am now

       is not what I will become.

What I will become

       Is yet to be determined.

Dear Dewey,

It has come to my attention that if I ever make these ponderings available to the greater reading public, a teacher who is new to the profession might happen upon these pages. It is with this thought in mind that I want to offer my observations as to a few types of newbies that I have seen over the recent years.

       In the broadest sense, I believe I can place teachers new to the profession in one of two categories. The first group is made up of enthusiastic, idealistic educators who long to make a difference in students' lives, but are quickly discouraged by a number of factors that they are sure to encounter. The first point of discouragement might come from the bureaucracy that is education. This will likely come in many forms, such as new initiatives from higher ups, endless paperwork, documentation, and record keeping, as well as obtaining updated curriculum and supplies. Just this year, I wanted a misplaced cable outlet in my room moved over ten feet. I put in for a work order and was told that a contractor would have to be hired, and for that to happen, I needed to get pre-approval from my principal since the monies to do such a job would come out of our site funds. Knowing this would take months, and I needed access to my ceiling mounted projector on a daily basis, I came up with my own solution, spending twenty dollars of my own money. Still, the job got done, and for less money and time than the district would have had to expend.

The second discouragement for the newbie might come from the students. Many educators love the school environment and are life-long learners. Not all, but many, were decent students during their K-12 years. So it is when they are faced with 150 students, many of whom don't share the enthusiasm for learning that their new teacher

243

does, it can be confusing and heart-wrenching for the newbie. I have lost count to how many times I heard the concern, "I don't get it. They don't seem to even care; like they don't want to learn. When I was their age, I loved school."

The last point of discouragement for our first group of newbies comes from their own undoing. Despite being told countless times that the students need a teacher, not a buddy, so many of the impressionable, well-meaning newbies will slip into the buddy mode. It never goes well. Students see it as a weakness and will exploit it for all it's worth. I get it; it's human nature to desire to be liked. In my first year I was determined not to make this mistake. I was 21 years old. Let's just say, it wasn't my best year.

The other significant group of newbies is also made up of enthusiastic, idealistic educators who long to make a difference in students' lives, but unlike the first, they navigate the seas of discouragement like an old mariner. It isn't that they aren't hit by the above mentioned bureaucracy, or unmotivated students, but there is something in the DNA of this group that, though they have a genuine passion for their subject matter and for their students, they have a steadier demeanor than the first group. The first group is like Mayor Vaughn in the *Jaws* movies, barely keeping his head above the fray as he tries to do his job, and everyone wonders if he'll make it. The second group is like the old fisherman, Quint, who straps in to the chair to go mano a mano with the great white shark. (Sure, Vaughn survives and is mayor in *Jaws 2*, and Quint is devoured in the movie, but you get the point.)

Dear Dewey,

The plight of the newbies continues to occupy my thoughts. In the spirit of wanting to see both groups succeed, allow me to pass on a couple of teacher nuggets that I have picked up over the years. Take what is helpful, discard what is not.

In my first teaching assignment, I was told by the principal, "Don't smile until November." That seemed fairly harsh to me. I didn't want to be "that" teacher that the students referred to as "the mean teacher." This is really just a different angle of "the students don't need you to be their buddy" adage. I'll smile before November, but I have come to know the faulty thinking of being their buddy. It really is detrimental to everyone. Be genuinely concerned for your students; the rest will take care of itself.

Bathroom breaks. If you are a coffee drinker as I am, you will learn how to best pace your intake. Depending on when your prep period is, finding a couple minutes to use the bathroom can be tricky. At my current site, if I am going to go to the bathroom between classes, I have to wait until the last class leaves, lock the door, make my way through the crowded halls so that I can walk half way across the campus to the Main Office, take care of business, then get back through the crowds to my room—all in 5 minutes from start to finish. No easy feat, but I can do it. Just be sure not to make eye contact or strike up a conversation with any faculty members during that time. You should also know who your campus homies are, so you can call them on their prep to come watch your class in case of an unscheduled emergency. You think I'm kidding, but this can save you from a huge embarrassing moment with your students.

Grading papers. This is a required part of the job, but not all assignments need to be graded with the same intensity. Depending on what you teach, and what type of assignments you give, there are usually alternatives to the traditional, "Teacher grading mountains of assignments at home." Talk with others in your department about what they do. Maybe just focus on an aspect of the assignment. Only grade a selection of problems you gave. Do some peer grading as you direct. The point is, you need to protect your "down time" with your spouse, family, friends, boyfriend/girlfriend, your dog, etc.

Mental health days. This is connected with the last point. Most schools give you ten paid days off, usually divided over things like sick days, personal necessity days, family care, and other such days. They used to have a couple days designated as "mental health days." This sounds like a clever way of saying, "Playing Hooky Day." I suppose in some ways it is, but the intended purpose is to give your brain and stressors a break. You do no one any good (you, your household, and your students) if you are burnt out. Currently, most newbies drop out of the profession within the first five years. There are many reasons for this, but burn-out is a major cause.

Sub plans. Also connected with the last one in some instances. There is an art to creating plans for a substitute. First, give as many details as possible, but know the sub may or may not follow them as you have explained. Just make sure if they don't, it's not because you left horrible plans. Second, try to structure the assignment so that it will be easy to grade when you get back, if at all. There's nothing like coming back from being sick, or from a mental health day, only to be overwhelmed by the amount of grading you need to do. Finally, make up one or two "emergency lesson plans" that you can keep in your desk or file cabinet. This way, if you wake up sick one morning, you already have plans ready to go. Make these generic enough to be used at any time during the school year.

Main Office Secretary. Most schools have a central figure in the Main Office. No not the principal. I'm talking about the person who keeps the school running on a day-to-day basis. Nowadays they might be called the Office Manager, or something like that. Be kind to her (it could be a male, but in every school I have been in, it has been a woman). If you need something, gently and humbly ask for her help, or that she can point you in the direction of where to get that help. You will have many needs, and there is no reason to get one of your greatest allies posturing against you. Note: other office personnel like counselors, registrar, and the attendance clerk should also be on your list of those to cultivate a positive relationship at all costs.

Class uniqueness. If you teach middle or high school, you will have numerous classes with numerous students. Even if you teach the same class all day long, each class will have their own personality. Morning classes will be significantly different from those after lunch. Smaller classes will not resemble larger classes. That lesson plan you designed to be exactly the same over five periods will come out varied. You will have a "favorite" class, but try not to let that be shown or known.

Change. My last tidbit to share for now has to do with change. The students you get in August will not be the same students you say goodbye to in June. Sure, they will largely be the same on paper, but the students will change, more times than not for the better. Some years I have found my students don't get into a groove, or that "fun phase," until after Christmas Break at the start of the second semester. Hang in there; they won't always be this obnoxious.

Dear Dewey,

As I bring this diary to a close, the words from Holy Scripture come to mind. "There is a way that seems right to a man, but in the end leads to destruction" (Proverbs 14:12). Now, while this may be a warning to those who will choose to go their own way over and against the way of the Lord, it seems to resonate with me at this moment. As I look over these pages and the events of the last year, I can't help but be reflective. I have chosen a path that seemed right to me, at least at the time. I pray that most of those choices were not knowingly against the will of my Creator, nor do I desire that they will lead to destruction for me or my students. I am a simple man, and a teacher by trade. Some would say by calling, but that seems a bit self-aggrandizing.

I have taken the time to write the thoughts contained on these pages as a means of self-care. I needed a place to express what was inside. These events in most cases involved other people. I didn't always agree with, or get along with, the folks mentioned, but that doesn't mean I do not care about them. We are all striving to make our way through this thing called life. As humans, we are going to bump into each other, maybe causing a bruise here and there, but that's what it means to be human. I am thankful for my fellow teachers, the administrators who work countless hours, often well into the evening and the support staff both on campus and from the district office. We are a motley crew, but we are a team. Whatever pain is reflected on these pages I know is shared by you, too.

.

Extra Credit

Dear Dewey,

I was grilling some burgers for my wife and me tonight. As I was putting the old cover back on, I noticed it had become cracked in spots due to weathering, a bit misshapen, and not nearly as flexible as it used to be. Then it struck me ... It was like I was looking in a mirror.

Dear Dewey,

They say you can't teach an old dog new tricks, but sometimes the old tricks are just too much for the old dog. As our beagle, Zack, enters his "golden years" I am seeing some of his previous guilty pleasures eroding. While he can still manage to get up on the couch for a nap, the two and a half foot jump up onto our bed is just too much for the old boy. I know how he feels. I wouldn't be able to make it, either, except I'm working with gravity instead of against it as I fall into bed every night. How I love that old hound.

Dear Dewey,

A few weeks ago I spotted a black widow spider in one corner of my garage. I had a can of insecticide on hand (specifically for spiders) and doused it. It shriveled instantly; on her back, legs curled into her body. A few days later I was walking by that spot and noticed a second black widow curled about a quarter inch away from the first. I figured either the residual of the spray got her, or she tried to eat the first and died. I felt smugly proud of myself. This repeated itself a couple more times until a week later when there were a total of four dead spiders in a row. This exceeded my greatest expectations for a bug spray. Well, today I walked by my trophy corner to find all four spider corpses gone. Vanished. Should I be concerned?

Dear Dewey,

After not having it for over ten years, we broke down and added basic cable to our internet package. I just came into the room and found my wife watching The Lawrence Welk Show. I'm sure ol' Larry and the other performers were all very nice people, but I'm not sure this was worth the wait. I think I'll just go back into the other room and read my AARP magazine.

Dear Dewey,

My back has been very sore over the last couple of weeks. I think it's from standing too much while I lecture. I decided to go to a chiropractor for the first time ever in my life. He says I have the back/spine of a 30 year old; a 30 year old mountain gorilla, that is.

Dear Dewey

Some days I just want to shout to the world, "There's still a lot of candy left in this pinata."

Dear Dewey,

I had to take the day off as I had an appointment at the dermatologist. In the waiting room was posted a sign that read, "Try to limit sun exposure to only twenty minutes a day." Twenty minutes a day? Really? What are we, vampires?

Dear Dewey,

Today around 12:30 pm, as I was wrapping up my 5th period class, I received a message from the principal of the elementary school near our house (about 45 miles from where I work). In short, our beagle, Zack, got out and made his way over to the school. The principal was calling to let me know that they had wrangled him in, and Zack was sitting comfortably in her office; water and doggy treats provided. (She called animal control. Based off the info on his tags, they were able to give her my cell number and our home address). When her school was over at 3 pm, she brought him back to our house. Man, I love this town!

Dear Dewey,

It's the weekend. I had dog-poop clean-up duty in the backyard today.

Can someone explain to me how one measured cup of dog food

becomes three cups (unmeasured) of dog waste?